Usborne Start to Cook

Abigail Wheatley

Designed & illustrated by Nancy Leschnikoff
Steps illustrated by Mark Ruffle & Non Figg

Photography by Howard Allman
Food preparation by Dagmar Vesely
Recipe consultants: Catherine Atkinson & Monita Buchwald
American editor: Carrie Armstrong

Contents

Bread & pastry

Cookies & cakes

You can find the recipe for these quick and delicious tomato tarts on page 150.

Using this book

This book is designed for anyone who's just starting out in the kitchen. It's full of tasty recipes explained in a clear and simple way. The first few pages show you how to get the most out of this book and give you some basic cooking tips. Then, you can just get cooking!

These tabs will help you to find your way around the different sections of the book.

At the start of each section are two introductory pages. These will give you some help with cooking the recipes in that section.

Step-by-step instructions explain some of the cooking methods you will come across in the recipes in each section.

Here you'll find useful hints about preparing and cooking the food in this section.

Nut allergies

Nuts are usually marked as optional in the ingredients lists, along with other foods that might be unsuitable for nut allergy sufferers. You'll also find a list of recipes containing nuts in the index.

In the introduction to each recipe, you'll find out about it. Sometimes, you'll find allergy advice, too.

The ingredients and particular equipment you need are listed here. You can also find how much the recipe makes, and there's sometimes allergy information here, too.

These steps show you what to do at each stage of the recipe.

Boxes like this contain suggestions for ways you can alter the main recipe to leave out ingredients you can't eat or don't like, or just to try something a little different.

A photo shows you how the recipe looks when it's cooked.

At the end of the book you'll find advice about eating a balanced diet and ways to adapt recipes for allergies. There's an Allergy Index too. It lists recipes containing nuts, and also shows you where to look for wheat- and gluten-free, dairy-free and egg-free options.

Getting started

Before you start cooking, it's useful to know about a few basics, such as how to measure out ingredients and what equipment to use.

First things first

Read through the recipe to make sure you have all the ingredients and equipment you will need before you start. Wash your hands before you begin. And when you've finished, don't forget to clean up your workspace.

Oven ready

Unless a recipe says otherwise, everything should be cooked on the middle shelf of the oven. Arrange the shelves before you turn on the oven.

Some ovens may cook things more quickly or slowly than the recipe says. If you have a convection oven, shorten the cooking time or lower the temperature a little. Your oven manual will help you.

Mixed salad leaves

Peeled red onions

Measuring

You will need an assortment of measuring cups and spoons to measure the ingredients in the recipes. Small amounts are measured with spoons. The ingredients should lie level with the top of the spoon.

A pinch of salt

'A pinch' is the amount you can pick up between your thumb and your first finger.

Some recipes include a pinch of salt. Others don't, as there's enough in other ingredients such as bouillon cubes. You can always add more salt when the food is on your plate.

Serving sizes

Each recipe tells you how many people the food will serve, or how many items it will make. Most of the recipes in this book are for 4 people. If you're cooking for 2, halve the recipe, or double it if you're cooking for 8. But for cakes and cookies it's best just to make the quantity the recipe says.

Some of the recipes in this book are complete meals in themselves; others have suggestions for things that could be eaten with them. If you need inspiration for side dishes, you could look at the pages on salads, potato salads, or the 'About...' spreads for rice, potatoes and vegetables.

Substituting

Most of the recipes in this book have suggestions for ways you could change them. Once you've got the hang of a recipe, you could try out your own ideas too – though it's best not to be experimental with baking, as the recipes might not work.

Kitchen safety

Here are a few simple safety tips to keep in mind when you're cooking.

Protect yourself

Food and equipment can get very hot. Protect your hands with oven mitts, especially when you're getting things in and out of the oven.

Ask for help

If you're going to use new equipment, such as a blender, for the first time, or if you're trying out something new, make sure you know what you're doing. If in doubt, ask someone with cooking experience to help you.

Chop safely

When you're cutting with a sharp knife, always use a cutting board to stop the food from slipping around. The recipe will tell you the safest way to cut things.

Hot pans

Be careful not to leave saucepan handles hanging over the front of the stove. Turn them to the side, so you don't knock them off. Move hot pans carefully so you don't spill the contents.

Keep watch

Don't leave the kitchen while you've got anything cooking on the stove or in the oven. Make sure you remember to turn off the heat when you've finished.

Clean up

It's a good idea to wipe up any spills on the floor, so you don't slip. If you keep the kitchen fairly neat as you cook, it makes it easier to keep track of where you are in the recipe, and helps when it comes to cleaning up afterward.

Fruit & vegetables

Cook classic dishes like
ratatouille, a vegetable stew.

Find out how to prepare
fruit and vegetables and make
them into delicious dishes..

To remove redcurrants from their stem, run a fork down the stem.

About fruit

Whether you're putting together a fruit salad or cooking a crumble, you often need to prepare the fruit first. Here are some useful tips and techniques.

Choosing fruit

Ripe fruit is often sweeter and softer than unripe fruit, so buy ripe fruit if you can. Or, ripen it at home by leaving it at room temperature.

Washing fruit

If you're going to eat the peel of fresh fruits, rinse the fruits under cold running water. Put smaller fruits, such as berries, cherries and grapes, in a strainer first.

Most citrus fruits are sold with a wax coating. If you're cooking with the zest or peel, scrub the fruits in warm water with a drop of dish liquid to remove the wax. Then, rinse and dry the fruits.

Added sugar

Some dried fruits, such as apples and cherries, and some canned fruits, may have sugar added. It's best to avoid these types if you're trying to cut down on sugar. Check the labels and choose natural dried fruits and canned fruits in natural fruit juice.

Dried tropical fruits sometimes have extra sugar added. It will say on the packaging.

Cutting up an apple

1 Cut the apple in half, then put the halves flat side down and cut them in half again. Use a peeler to peel the skin off the quarters.

2 Take a quarter. Cut away from you, at a slant, to halfway under the core. Turn the quarter around and make another cut in the same way.

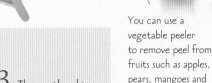

You can use a vegetable peeler to remove peel from fruits such as apples, pears, mangoes and kiwi fruit.

Cutting up an orange

1 Cut the orange into slices around the same thickness as your finger.

2 Put each slice flat on the cutting board and slice off the skin and all the white part underneath it.

3 Throw the skin away. Then, cut up the orange slices into small pieces.

These curls of lemon rind were made using a tool called a zester.

Grating citrus zest

Scrape the outside of the fruit across the small holes of a grater. Try not to grate off the white part just under the zest.

Squeezing citrus fruit

Cut the fruit in half. Hold the cut side of one half on a citrus squeezer. Turn it around, pressing and squeezing. Do the same with the other half.

This lemon has had its zest removed with a zester.

Preparing fruit with pits

1 Slide a knife in until the point touches the central pit. Move the knife all the way around the fruit, following the pit.

2 Pull apart the two halves and remove the pit. Cut the fruit into pieces.

Use your fingers to pull the green leaves and stems from strawberries — or cut them out if the fruit is hard.

Fruit smoothies

Ingredients:

2 oranges

¾ cup raspberries

1 small banana

1 teaspoon of honey

Makes 1 smoothie

Your smoothies will blend more easily, and taste better, if you use ripe fruits.

This recipe shows how to make smoothies by hand. If you have a food processor, you can make them even smoother – just remove any stalks or thick skin, put in all the ingredients and blend until smooth. This recipe is for a raspberry and orange smoothie.

1 Squeeze the juice from the oranges. Wash the raspberries in a strainer under cold running water and shake them dry. If you don't mind a few seeds in your smoothie, put the raspberries in a wide pitcher and skip to step 3.

Strawberry & pineapple smoothie

You will need 1 cup strawberries, 1 small banana and ⅔ cup pineapple juice.

Remove the green stems from the strawberries and peel the banana. Put the fruits in a wide pitcher and mash until smooth. Add the pineapple juice and mix.

Blackberry & apple smoothie

You will need ¾ cup blackberries, 1 small banana, ⅔ cup apple juice and 1 tablespoon of plain yogurt.

Prepare the blackberries in the same way as the raspberries in steps 1-2 above. Follow step 3, leaving out the honey. Add the yogurt and apple juice and mix.

2 For a really smooth smoothie, use the back of a spoon to push the raspberries through a strainer into a wide pitcher. Scrape any pulp off the back of the strainer and put that in the pitcher, too.

3 Peel the banana and put it in the pitcher. Add the honey. Use a fork or a potato masher to mash and squash the fruits and honey, until you have a smooth mixture.

4 Use a fork to mix in the orange juice. Continue mixing until the smoothie is slightly frothy.

Banana & vanilla smoothie

You will need 1 large banana, 1 teaspoon of honey, ½ teaspoon of vanilla extract, ¼ cup of plain yogurt and ⅔ cup milk.

Put the peeled banana, honey and vanilla in a pitcher. Mash the banana until it is smooth. Stir in the yogurt, then mix in the milk.

Orange & banana smoothie

You will need 2 oranges, 1 large banana and 1 teaspoon of honey.

Squeeze the juice from the oranges. Follow steps 3-4 above. You could use 5 clementines or tangerines instead of the oranges, if you prefer.

Tropical fruit skewers

Ingredients:

3 tablespoons of honey

2 limes

²/₃ cup plain yogurt (optional)

an 8oz. can of pineapple chunks
  or slices in natural fruit juice

1 large ripe banana

1 large ripe firm nectarine

4 teaspoons of sugar

You will also need 8 long or 16 short
  barbecue skewers

Serves 4

Other fruits

You could use strawberries
or canned pears or peaches
instead. To prepare the
strawberries, wash them
and remove the green
stems. Prepare the peaches
or pears the same way
as the pineapple
in step 4.

In this recipe, you put fruit on barbecue skewers and grill it. This cooks the natural sugars in the fruit, making it taste extra sweet.

1 If you're using wooden skewers, put them into a pan of water to soak. This helps to stop them from burning when you put them in the broiler.

2 Put the honey in a small bowl. Grate the rind from the limes using the small holes on a grater. Cut the limes in half and squeeze out the juice. Put the juice and rind in the bowl.

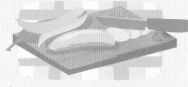

3 Mix the juice and honey. Put half the mixture in a large bowl. Put the yogurt in the small bowl. Mix it in. Peel the banana, cut it into bite-sized chunks and put it in the large bowl.

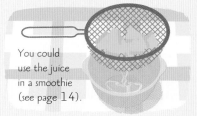

You could
use the juice
in a smoothie
(see page 14).

4 Open the can of pineapple and pour the contents into a strainer to drain. If you're using pineapple slices, cut them into bite-sized chunks. Put the pineapple in the large bowl.

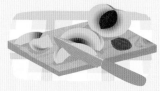

5 Cut the nectarine in half and remove the pit. Cut the nectarine into thick slices. Cut the slices into chunks.

6 Put the nectarine chunks in the large bowl with the rest of the fruit. Stir it all together and leave it for a few minutes.

7 Put a piece of fruit on a board. Push the point of a skewer into it. Move the fruit up the skewer. Add more fruit in the same way, until you fill the skewers.

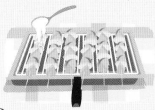

8 Turn the broiler to a high temperature and leave it to heat up for 3-4 minutes. Meanwhile, arrange the skewers on the broiler pan. Sprinkle half the sugar over them.

9 Broil the skewers for 3-4 minutes. Then, turn them over and sprinkle over the rest of the sugar. Broil for another 3-4 minutes.

10 Let the skewers cool for 2-3 minutes. To eat the fruit, hold a skewer upright with the point on your plate, and pull each piece of fruit down and off with your fork.

You could sprinkle some grated lime zest over the yogurt, if you like.

Apple berry crisp

Ingredients:

For the crisp topping:

1 cup whole-wheat flour

½ teaspoon of ground cinnamon

½ stick (¼ cup) butter, margarine or dairy free spread

½ cup old-fashioned (rolled) oats, or unsalted nuts such as hazelnuts, almonds or pistachios (optional)

¼ cup sugar

For the fruit filling:

2 cups fresh or frozen blackberries, blueberries or raspberries

1 orange

1lb. sweet apples

1 tablespoon of sugar

You will also need an ovenproof pan

Serves 4

This crisp makes a warming dessert for a cold day. The apples and berries create a soft and tangy filling, while the cinnamon and oats or nuts in the topping make it slightly spiced and crunchy.

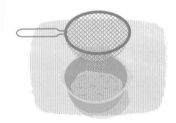

1 Preheat the oven to 350°F. Sift the flour and cinnamon into a large bowl. Pour in any bits of bran from the flour that are left in the strainer, too.

2 Cut up the butter, margarine or spread into small chunks. Put them in the bowl. Use your fingers and thumbs to mix the butter into the flour, until the mixture looks like small breadcrumbs (see page 149).

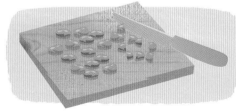

3 If you're using nuts, put them on a board and chop them into small pieces. Put the chopped nuts or the oats in the bowl and add the sugar, too. Stir everything together.

5 Put the apples on a cutting board and cut each one in half. Put the halves flat side down and cut them in half again. Use a peeler to peel the skin off the quarters.

4 Wash the berries in a strainer and shake them dry. Put them in the ovenproof dish. Cut the orange in half and squeeze out the juice. Put the juice in the pan with the berries.

6 Take a quarter. Make a slanting cut to halfway under the core. Turn the quarter around and make another cut in the same way. Do this to all the quarters.

7 Throw away the cores. Cut the apple into bite-sized chunks. Put them in the pan with the berries. Add the sugar and mix.

8 Spoon the topping over the fruits. Put the pan on a cookie sheet to catch any drips and put it in the oven for 35 minutes, or until the top is browned.

Apple or pear crisp

If you want to make a crisp using only apples, or using pears, just follow the main recipe, leaving out the berries. You will need 1½lbs. sweet apples or pears.

Quick fruit crisp

You can adapt the main recipe to make a quick filling, using a 14oz. can of pear halves, peach slices or other fruits, instead of the apples and orange. Follow steps 1-3 of the main recipe, then open the can and pour the fruit and juice into a strainer over a bowl. Chop the fruits into bite-sized chunks and put them in your pan. Spoon in 4 tablespoons of juice. You won't need to add any sugar. Mix in the berries, then follow step 8.

Fresh lemonade

Ingredients:

4 lemons, preferably unwaxed

1 cup sugar

cold water, or selzer

a few ice cubes

Makes around 12 glasses

This recipe shows you how to make old-fashioned lemonade that tastes deliciously of real lemons. Make it with chilled plain water, or use sparkling water to make it fizzy.

1 Use a vegetable peeler to peel the zest from the lemons in thin strips. Try to peel off just the yellow zest and not the bitter white pith underneath.

2 Put the zest in a saucepan with 1 cup water. Put the pan on very low heat. When the water boils, put on a lid. Let the water bubble gently for 5 minutes. Turn off the heat.

4 Cut the lemons in half and squeeze out all the juice. Pour the juice through a strainer into a large pitcher. Pour the cooled sugar syrup through the strainer as well, then throw away the leftover lemon zest.

3 Add the sugar to the pan and stir until it has dissolved completely. Then, take the pan off the heat and leave it to cool.

If you can't get unwaxed fruit, scrub them in warm water with a drop of dish liquid, to remove the wax (see page 12).

You can keep the undiluted syrup in the refrigerator for up to a week in a sealed container.

5 Stir the syrup to mix it. Then, pour some syrup into a glass, filling it around a quarter full. Add a few ice cubes, then top up with chilled water, or sparkling water.

Orangeade

Limeade

To make a delicious, fresh limeade, simply follow the main recipe on the opposite page, using 6 limes instead of the lemons.

Raspberry lemonade

Extra ingredients: 1 cup fresh raspberries.
Follow steps 1-4 of the main recipe. Then, put the raspberries in the strainer over the pitcher. Squash them with the back of a spoon so all the juice goes through but the seeds stay behind. Use a spoon to scrape any raspberry pulp off the back of the strainer and put that in too. Then, follow step 5.

Orangeade

Use 4 oranges instead of the lemons. At step 3, add just ⅔ cup sugar, as oranges are naturally sweeter than lemons. Then, follow steps 4 and 5.

Raspberry lemonade

Lemonade

Fruit salad sundaes

Ingredients:

3 oranges

2 tablespoons of honey

1 cup fresh raspberries

3 ripe peaches

1¼ cups plain yogurt (optional)

For the raspberry sauce:

4 tablespoons of powdered sugar

1 cup fresh raspberries

You will also need 4 sundae-style serving glasses

Serves 4

Serving fresh fruit salad as a sundae turns it into an extra-special treat. The main recipe here uses peaches, oranges and raspberries, but there are plenty of other suggestions on the right to try, too.

1 Cut one of the oranges in half. Squeeze out the juice and put it in a large bowl. Add the honey and stir it in.

2 Cut the other oranges into thick slices. Put each slice flat on the cutting board and cut off the skin and white pith. Cut the orange into pieces and put them in the bowl.

3 Wash the raspberries in a strainer under cold running water, then shake them dry. Put them in the bowl with the orange pieces.

4 Wash the peaches. Cut them in half, then take out the pits. Then, cut the peach halves into bite-sized pieces and put them in the bowl. Mix the fruits together.

5 Spoon the fruits and juice into 4 sundae glasses. Then, spoon the yogurt on top, dividing it between the glasses.

6 To make the raspberry sauce, put the sugar in a strainer over a bowl. Sift it through and push any lumps through with the back of a spoon.

7 Put the raspberries in the strainer, wash them and shake them dry. Put them in the bowl with the sugar. Use a fork or a potato masher to mash the raspberries and sugar until you have a fairly smooth sauce. Mix the sauce well, then spoon it over the sundaes.

Raspberry & mandarin sundae

For a quick version of the main recipe, replace the oranges with an 11oz. can of mandarin segments in juice, and the peaches with a 15oz. can of peach slices.

Spoon the fruits into 4 dishes, add 2 tablespoons of juice to each glass, then follow steps 5-7.

Apple & cinnamon sundae

You will need 2 sweet apples, 2 pears, 8 tablespoons of apple juice, 1¼ cups plain yogurt, 4 tablespoons of honey and ¼ teaspoon of ground cinnamon.

Cut the fruits into pieces. Put them into 4 glasses. Add the apple juice, then the yogurt. Mix the cinnamon and honey. Drizzle over the top.

Banana & toffee sundae

You will need 2 ripe bananas, a 15oz. can of peach slices in juice, 1 cup fresh blueberries, 1¼ cups plain yogurt, and 6 tablespoons light brown sugar.

Slice the bananas. Put them in 4 glasses. Add some peach slices and 2 tablespoons of their juice to each glass. Mix in the blueberries. Top with the yogurt, then the sugar. Chill for 2 hours.

Kiwi & pineapple sundae

You will need 2 ripe bananas, 4 ripe kiwi fruits, a 15oz. can of pineapple pieces, 1¼ cups plain yogurt and 4 tablespoons of honey.

Peel and slice the bananas and the kiwi fruits. Divide them between 4 glasses. Add some pineapple pieces and 2 tablespoons of their juice to each glass. Put the yogurt on top and drizzle over the honey.

You could add some chopped nuts too, if you like.

21

Crunchy granola & fruit

Ingredients:

1 cup shelled, unsalted nuts such
   as hazelnuts or almonds (optional,
   see the opposite page)

2½ tablespoons of vegetable oil

5 tablespoons of honey

1 teaspoon of vanilla extract

3 cups old-fashioned (rolled) oats

½ cup sunflower seeds (optional)

2½ tablespoons of sesame seeds (optional)

⅔ cup dried fruits such as dried figs,
   dates, apricots or apples

⅓ cup raisins or golden raisins

Makes 12 helpings

In this recipe, oats are baked in the oven with a little oil and honey, making a toasted, crunchy breakfast cereal. Then you add lots of dried fruits. It's delicious served with chilled milk, or you could add it to yogurt and fresh fruit.

1 Preheat the oven to 350°F. Put the nuts in a clean plastic food bag and close the end. Roll a rolling pin over the nuts to crush them into pieces.

2 Put the vegetable oil, honey and vanilla in a saucepan. Put the pan over low heat. Stir the mixture until it is warm and runny. Then, turn off the heat.

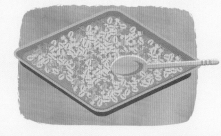

This granola recipe is perfect for making into granola bars. You'll find a delicious and easy recipe for chocolate granola bars on page 162.

3 Put the crushed nuts, oats, sunflower seeds and sesame seeds in the pan. Stir until the honey and oil coat the other ingredients.

4 Pour the mixture into a roasting pan. Spread it out in an even layer. Bake for 15 minutes, then take the pan out of the oven, mix everything around and put it back in the oven for another 10 minutes.

5 While the granola is in the oven, snip the figs, dates, apricots or other fruits into small pieces. When the granola is cooked, leave it to cool for 10 minutes. Then, stir in the chopped fruits and raisins.

6 Spoon the granola into a jar or plastic box and put on a lid. It will keep for 14 days. One serving is around 5 heaped tablespoons of granola.

Maple pecan granola

At step 1, simply replace the nuts with 1 cup unsalted pecans. Then, at step 2, replace the honey with 5 tablespoons of maple syrup and replace the vanilla extract with 2 teaspoons of ground cinnamon.

Berry cherry granola

At step 5, just replace the dried figs, dates or apricots with ⅔ cup dried berries such as blueberries, cranberries or cherries (or a mixture) and replace the raisins with ⅓ cup dried currants.

Nut-free granola

If you can't eat nuts or seeds, or you just don't like them, leave them out. Instead, you could add 1 cup extra oats, or ½ cup wheat germ and ½ cup oat or wheat bran. You can buy wheat germ and oat or wheat bran at health food stores.

A radish

A variety of
different mushrooms

Edamame
beans

A pea   A grape
tomato

About vegetables

You'll find instructions here that will help you to tackle most
common vegetables. There are also some tips on preparing salad
ingredients, too.

Washing vegetables

Scrub muddy vegetables under cold running
water. If you can't get off all the mud, peel
them using a vegetable peeler. Most other types
of vegetables and salad ingredients can simply be
rinsed in cold water.

Frozen vegetables

Frozen vegetables are easy to use: just follow
the instructions printed on the packaging.

If you need to defrost frozen vegetables,
spread them on a plate and leave them at room
temperature for half an hour or so.

Boiling or steaming vegetables

Cut up large vegetables into bite-sized pieces. To boil them, put a pan of cold water on
medium heat. When the water boils, turn the heat down so it's boiling gently. Lower in
the vegetables. To steam them, put a pan a third full of water over medium heat. Put a
steamer or colander on top and put in the prepared vegetables. Put a lid on the steamer
or colander. Cook until the vegetables are tender when you poke them with a knife.

Green onions

Red onion

Red bell pepper

Different types of tomatoes

You don't need to peel baby carrots like these.

A bulb of garlic

This is one clove. Peel off the papery skin, then crush it using a garlic crusher.

Chopping an onion

1 Cut the top and the hairy root off the onion and throw them away. Then, peel off the outer layer of papery skin and discard it.

2 Cut the onion in half. Put the halves flat on the board and cut them into thin slices.

3 Some recipes also ask you to cut the slices into small pieces. Put them flat on the board before you chop them.

Green onions

Cut off the roots and most of the dark green parts. Cut or snip up the rest.

Preparing bell peppers

1 Cut the top off the bell pepper and throw it away. Cut the pepper in half.

2 Pull out the seeds and white parts. Discard them. Then, cut up the pepper.

Preparing avocados

1 Cut the avocado in half from top to bottom, cutting around the central pit.

2 Use a spoon to scoop out the pit. Peel off the skin, then cut up the avocado.

Big tomatoes

Cut big tomatoes into quarters. Cut out the green core from each quarter.

Peeling vegetables

Hold the vegetable firmly. Scrape a vegetable peeler across the skin again and again. Be careful not to scrape your fingers.

Dips & salsas

Ingredients:

3 large carrots

1 lemon

2½ tablespoons of olive oil

2 teaspoons of ground cumin

1 teaspoon of ground coriander seed

½ teaspoon of ground cinnamon

½ teaspoon of paprika

Serves 4

Dips and salsas are great foods for snacks, lunches or parties. The main recipe here is for a tasty carrot dip, but on the right there are others dips, and a salsa to try, too.

1 Peel the carrots and cut off the tops. Cut the carrots into chunks and put them in a saucepan. Cover them with cold water. Put a lid on the pan and put it on medium heat.

2 When the water starts to boil, turn down the heat, so it boils gently. Cook for 15-20 minutes, until the carrots are really soft. Test one by poking the point of a sharp knife into it.

3 Put the cooked carrots in a colander to drain and cool. While the carrots are cooling, cut the lemon in half and squeeze out all the juice.

4 If you don't have a blender, skip to step 5. If you do, put in the carrots, lemon juice, olive oil, cumin, coriander, cinnamon and paprika. Add a pinch of salt and some pepper. Blend until you have a smooth dip.

5 If you're blending your dip by hand, put the cooled carrots back in the pan. Mash them with a potato masher until they are as smooth as you can manage.

6 Add the lemon juice, olive oil, cumin, cilantro, cinnamon, paprika, some pepper and a pinch of salt. Mix to make a smooth dip.

Tomato salsa

You will need ½ red onion, 6 medium-sized ripe tomatoes, the juice of 1 lime and 6 sprigs of cilantro.

Cut the half onion into very small pieces. Quarter the tomatoes and chop them into very small pieces. Put them in a bowl with the onion and lime juice. Chop the cilantro leaves and mix them in. Add a few drops of hot pepper sauce, if you like.

Beet dip

Replace the carrots with 7-9oz. vacuum-packed or canned cooked beets. You will also need a blender.

Cut the beets into chunks and put them in the blender with the lemon juice, olive oil, spices, a pinch of salt and some pepper. Blend to a smooth dip.

Guacamole

You will need 2 ripe avocados, the juice of 1 lime, 1 clove of garlic and 4 teaspoons of olive oil.

Prepare the avocados, cut them into small pieces and put them in a bowl. Mash them with a fork or potato masher. Add the lime juice and put it in the bowl. Crush in the garlic and add the olive oil. Mix well. You could add a few drops of hot pepper sauce, if you like.

Tsatsiki

You will need a piece of cucumber around 4 inches long, 2 sprigs of mint, 1 small clove of garlic (optional) and 1¼ cups plain yogurt.

Grate the cucumber on the big holes of a grater. Put it in a strainer over the sink. Sprinkle over a pinch of salt. Snip the mint leaves into tiny pieces. Squeeze out the cucumber and put it in a bowl. Crush in the garlic, add the mint and some pepper. Stir in the yogurt.

Salads

Ingredients:

1 head butter lettuce

3 medium-sized ripe tomatoes

1 red or yellow bell pepper

1 small carrot

You may also need a small jar
with a tightly fitting lid

Serves 4

Salads are very versatile — you can add or take away
ingredients and choose whichever dressing you prefer.
This recipe is for a mixed salad. You'll find others opposite.

1 Pull all the leaves off the lettuce. Rinse
them in cold water, then put them in a clean
dishtowel and gather the edges together.
Shake it over the sink, to dry the lettuce.
Then, break the lettuce leaves into pieces.

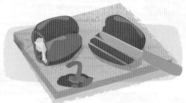

2 If you're using very small tomatoes, cut them in
half. Cut larger ones into quarters and cut out the
green core from each piece, like this.

3 Cut the top off the bell pepper. Cut the bell pepper in half
and pull out all the seeds and white parts. Cut each half into
slices about as thick as a pencil.

4 Scrub or peel the carrot and grate it on
the large holes of a grater. Then, put the
lettuce, tomatoes, pepper and carrot
in a large bowl.

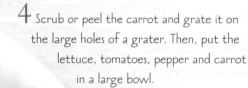

5 Choose a dressing from the
opposite page and make it by following
the instructions there. Pour the dressing
over the salad. Mix the salad, using your
hands or salad servers.

Coleslaw

You will need ¼ head of white or red cabbage, ½ lemon or lime, 1 large sweet apple, 1 large carrot and ½ red onion, plus a dressing.
Cut any hard stems from the cabbage. Slice the cabbage finely. Squeeze the juice from the half lemon or lime. Quarter the apple. Remove the cores. Grate the apple on the big holes of a grater, put it in a bowl with the lemon juice and mix. Grate the carrot on the big holes of a grater. Chop the onion finely. Put the carrot, cabbage, onion and dressing in the bowl and mix.

Green salad

You will need 1½ cups frozen peas, 4 green onions, a ripe avocado, 7oz. mixed salad leaves and a dressing.
Spread the peas on a plate to defrost. Follow step 1. Snip the white and pale green parts of the green onions into small pieces and put them in the bowl. Cut the avocado flesh into slices. Add the salad leaves, defrosted peas and dressing, and mix.

Tomato salad

You will need around 1lb. ripe tomatoes, 2½ tablespoons of olive oil and 2 sprigs of fresh basil.
Leave the tomatoes at room temperature for an hour or two. This will make them taste sweeter. Then, cut them into bite-sized chunks and cut out any large green cores. Put the tomatoes on a plate. Sprinkle over a pinch of salt, then drizzle on the olive oil. Tear the basil leaves into small pieces and scatter them on top.

Mayonnaise dressing

Mix 5 tablespoons of mayonnaise and 6 tablespoons of plain yogurt.

Honey mustard dressing

Put 5 tablespoons of olive oil, 4 teaspoons of balsamic or wine vinegar, 1 teaspoon of wholegrain or Dijon mustard and 1 teaspoon of honey in a jar. Put on the lid and shake to mix the ingredients.

Chili lime dressing

Put the juice of 1 lime, 4 tablespoons of olive oil, 1 tablespoon of sweet chili sauce (or, if unavailable, a few drops of mild chili sauce), 1 tablespoon of wine vinegar and 1 teaspoon of sugar in a jar. Put on the lid and shake to mix.

Pea & mint soup

Ingredients:

1 vegetable bouillon cube

1 onion

1 medium-sized potato

1½ tablespoons butter, margarine
  or dairy-free spread

1 clove of garlic

3 cups frozen peas

a few sprigs of fresh mint

a little plain yogurt (optional)

Serves 4

Carrot & cilantro

Replace the peas with
1lb. carrots and the mint
with a few sprigs of
fresh cilantro.
Follow steps 1-3. Then,
prepare the carrots and cut
them into chunks the same size
as the potato. Follow step 4.
In step 5, add the carrots at
the same time as the
potato. Follow step 6.
In step 7, use the
cilantro instead of
the mint. Follow
steps 8-10.

This pea soup is very quick and easy to cook, and it doesn't matter whether or not you use a blender – either way, it's delicious. You don't have to include the fresh herbs, but they make it taste more interesting and look pretty, too.

1 Put the bouillon cube in a heat-proof measuring cup. Add 3 cups boiling water. Stir until it dissolves.

2 Peel the onion, trim off the ends and cut it in half. Cut the halves into quarters and the quarters into thin slices. Then, cut the slices into small pieces.

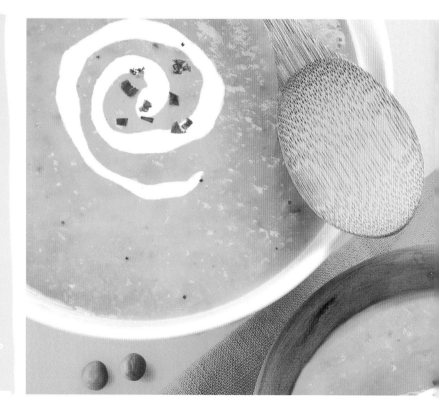

3 Peel the potato using a vegetable peeler. Then, cut it into large chunks around 1 inch across.

4 Put the butter in a saucepan. Put the pan on medium heat until the butter has melted. Put the onion in the pan and cook it for 5 minutes, stirring now and then.

5 Crush the garlic into the pan. Cook for 1 more minute, stirring all the time. The onion should have softened. Put the potato in the pan, then add the bouillon and some pepper.

6 When the soup starts to boil, turn down the heat so it bubbles gently. Put on a lid, leaving a small gap, and cook for 10 minutes. Then add the peas and cook for 10 more minutes.

7 While the soup is cooking, pick the mint leaves off their stalks. Put the leaves in a cup. Snip them into small pieces using kitchen scissors.

8 When the soup is cooked, leave it to cool for a few minutes. If you have a food processor, ladle in the soup and blend until smooth, then skip to step 10. If you don't have one, follow the next step.

9 To blend the soup by hand, pour it into a strainer over a large bowl. Put the vegetables back in the pan and mash with a potato masher. Pour the liquid back into the pan and mix.

10 Re-heat the soup over gentle heat for a few minutes. Then, ladle it into bowls, sprinkle over the chopped herbs and add a spoonful of yogurt.

Tomato sauce

Ingredients:

2 cloves of garlic

1 tablespoon of olive oil

a 14oz. can of diced tomatoes

2½ tablespoons of tomato paste

1 pinch of sugar

12 fresh basil leaves

Serves 4

You make this tomato sauce with canned tomatoes, garlic and fresh basil. It's easy and can be used in lots of different ways. Eat it on pasta and pizza, or as a sauce for dipping garlic bread or mozzarella sticks. There are some variations below, so you can change the flavors to suit your taste.

1 Peel the garlic. Crush it into a saucepan. Add the olive oil, diced tomatoes, tomato paste, sugar, a pinch of salt and some pepper.

2 Put the pan on medium heat and cook for around 15 minutes, stirring often, until the sauce becomes really thick.

3 Take the basil leaves off their stalks. Tear the leaves into small pieces and stir them into the sauce.

Other herbs

Instead of fresh basil, you could use a few sprigs of fresh thyme. Pull the leaves off the stalks and just stir them straight into the sauce in step 3. If you don't have any fresh herbs, add half a teaspoon of dried oregano or Italian herb blend in step 1, at the same time as the salt and pepper.

Tomato & onion sauce

Extra ingredient: 1 large onion.

Peel the onion, cut off the ends and cut it in half. Cut the halves into thin slices and cut the slices into small pieces. Put the onion in a saucepan with the olive oil. Put the pan on medium heat, and cook, stirring every now and then, for around 5 minutes, or until the onion is soft. Then peel the garlic and crush it in, add the diced tomatoes, tomato paste, sugar, a pinch of salt and some pepper. Follow steps 2 and 3.

Spaghetti & meatballs with tomato sauce

Extra ingredients: 1 slice of bread (or gluten-free bread), 2½ tablespoons of milk (or soy milk), 1½ teaspoons of balsamic vinegar, ½ onion, 8oz. lean ground beef and 12oz. dried spaghetti (or allergy-free pasta).

1 Preheat the oven to 400°F. Then, wipe a little oil over a cookie sheet.

2 Tear up the bread and put it in a bowl with the milk and vinegar. Leave for 3 minutes, then mash it with a fork.

3 Chop the onion into tiny pieces and put them in the bowl. Add the meat, a pinch of salt and some pepper. Mix everything together with your hands.

4 Take off a small piece of the mixture, and roll it between the palms of your hands to make a meatball about the size of walnut. Make lots more. Put the meatballs on the cookie sheet and put it in the oven for 15-20 minutes.

5 Meanwhile, follow the main recipe to make the tomato sauce. While it's cooking, boil the spaghetti (see page 67).

6 When everything is cooked, drain the spaghetti and put it in the pan with the tomato sauce. Add the meatballs and mix. You could grate on some Parmesan, too.

Vegetable stir-fry

Ingredients:

a 1 inch piece of fresh ginger

1 small orange

1 tablespoon of soy sauce or wheat-
and gluten-free tamari sauce

1 tablespoon of honey

1 tablespoon of white wine vinegar

1 teaspoon of sesame oil (for those
with nut allergies, use vegetable oil)

8oz. broccoli

1 carrot

1 red or yellow bell pepper

a 5oz. can of whole baby corn

6 green onions

1 tablespoon of plain cooking oil such
as sunflower oil

½ cup cashew nuts (optional)

Serves 4

Stir-frying is a fast and easy way of cooking where you fry things quickly, stirring them all the time. The stir-fried vegetables in this recipe stay crisp and crunchy, and take on the tangy flavors of soy sauce, honey and orange juice.

1 Cut the brown skin off the ginger and throw it away. Grate the ginger on the small holes of your grater. Throw away any tough, stringy pieces that are hard to grate.

2 Squeeze the juice from the orange. Put the juice in a measuring cup. Add the grated ginger, soy sauce, honey, vinegar and the sesame oil (or vegetable oil), too. Mix well.

A wok like this one is just the right shape for stir-frying.

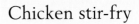

3 Cut the thick central stem off the broccoli and throw it away. Cut the rest into clumps and then into bite-sized pieces. Scrub or peel the carrot and cut it into thin strips.

4 Cut the top off the bell pepper and throw it away. Cut the bell pepper in half and pull out the seeds and white parts. Then, cut the rest into bite-sized chunks.

Chicken stir-fry

Extra ingredients:
1 tablespoon of vegetable oil and 3 skinless, boneless chicken breasts or thighs. Follow step 1. At step 2, put everything in a large bowl. Cut the chicken into bite-sized pieces and put them in the bowl. Follow steps 3-5. At step 6, before you add the vegetables, take the chicken out of the liquid and put it in the pan. Cook for 2-3 minutes, until it is brownish-white all over. Remove the chicken with a clean spoon and put it on a plate. Put the extra oil in the pan, heat for 20 seconds, then add the vegetables. At step 7, put the chicken back in the pan just before you add the orange juice mixture. Follow the rest of the instructions.

5 Drain the corn, then each piece in half lengthways. Cut the roots and most of the dark green parts off the green onions and throw them away. Cut the rest into thin slices.

6 Put the cooking oil in a large frying pan or wok. Put the pan on medium heat for 1 minute. Add the broccoli, carrot, corn and pepper.

You could eat your stir-fry with noodles or rice.

7 Cook for 2 minutes, stirring all the time. Then, add the green onions and cook for 1 minute, still stirring all the time. Pour in the orange juice mixture and stir everything together.

8 Turn up the heat to high and cook for 5 minutes, stirring all the time. Then, stir in the cashew nuts.

Ratatouille

Ingredients:

2 onions

2 zucchini

1 medium eggplant

3 red or yellow bell peppers

4 tablespoons of olive oil

2 cloves of garlic

2 x 14oz. cans of
  diced tomatoes

2½ tablespoons of tomato paste

1 teaspoon of dried oregano

8 large basil leaves

Serves 4

Ratatouille is a deliciously soft vegetable stew made with tomatoes, eggplants and other vegetables. You can serve it alongside a main dish such as roasted chicken (page 98), with baked potatoes (see page 80), or with fried eggs (see the page opposite) and crusty bread to mop up the juices.

It's best to make ratatouille in the summer. Eggplants, bell peppers and zucchini all need sun and warmth to grow and ripen, so that's when they're at their best, and are cheapest to buy.

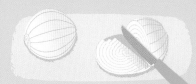

1 Peel the onions and cut off the ends. Cut the onions in half. Then, cut the halves into thin slices.

2 Cut the ends off the zucchini. Cut each zucchini in half lengthways. Then, cut the halves into strips and the strips into chunks.

3 Prepare the eggplants in the same way as the zucchini.

5 Put the oil and onions in a large saucepan. Put on low heat and cook the onions for about 10 minutes, until they are soft and starting to turn golden. Stir them every now and then.

4 Cut the end off each bell pepper and throw it away. Then, cut each bell pepper in half and each half in half again. Take out the seeds and white pith. Then, cut the rest into bite-sized chunks.

6 Peel the garlic and crush it into the pan. Then, add the diced tomatoes, the other vegetables, tomato paste, oregano and a pinch of salt and pepper. Stir well. Turn the heat to medium and cook for about 3 minutes.

7 Then, turn down the heat, so it bubbles gently. Cover the pan with a lid and cook for 10 minutes. Stir every now and then, watching out for the hot steam when you lift the lid. Then, remove the lid and cook for 40 minutes.

Ratatouille with eggs

Extra ingredients: 4-8 eggs and 5 tablespoons of cooking oil.

Follow steps 1-8. Fry the eggs following the instructions on page 57. Spoon some ratatouille onto 4 plates and slide the fried eggs on top. Tear up the basil leaves and scatter them on top.

8 Tear the basil leaves into small pieces and stir them into the ratatouille just before you serve it.

Roasted vegetables

Ingredients:

2 red onions

1lb. medium-sized potatoes
   or sweet potatoes,
   or a mixture

2 carrots

3 tablespoons of olive oil

1 tablespoon of honey

1 teaspoon of wholegrain
   mustard (optional)

Serves 4

These roasted vegetables can be served as a side dish for a roast chicken — or you could add a package of thickly sliced cheese at step 6, to make a meal in itself.

1 Put a roasting pan in the oven. Heat the oven to 400°F.

2 Peel the onions. Pull off any roots. Cut each onion in half, through the root. Then cut each half into three wedges, through the root.

3 Scrub or peel the potatoes and carrots. Cut them into ¾ inch thick slices. Put them in a bowl. Put the onion wedges in, too.

4 Put the olive oil in a cup. Add the honey and mustard and mix with a fork. Pour the mixture over the vegetables in the bowl. Mix everything together.

5 Take the pan out of the oven. Pour in the vegetables. Spread them out in a single layer, then bake for 40 minutes.

6 Wearing oven mitts, take the pan out of the oven. Turn the vegetables over. Then put them back in the oven for another 20 minutes.

Dairy & eggs

Cook light, airy biscuits, perfect to eat with preserves.

Find out how to whisk egg whites and make them into sweet meringues.

About dairy

Milk, and all the foods that are made from milk, are known as dairy products. This includes butter, yogurt, cream and cheese. You should store dairy products in the refrigerator.

Milk

Most milk comes from cows, but you can also buy milk from goats and sheep, and non-dairy milks made from things such as soybeans and nuts. When a recipe includes milk, it means cow's milk (unless it says otherwise). Full-fat is the creamiest. Reduced-fat and skim milk have had some cream removed: go for these types if you're watching how much fat you eat.

This is plain yogurt.

Whipped cream

Cream

Always use the type of cream a recipe says. Heavy and whipping cream can both be whipped, but heavy cream tastes a little richer. Light cream contains less fat, but you can't whip it.

Butter

Butter is made by beating milk until the watery part separates from the fat. The fat clumps together until it eventually forms a solid lump of butter.

Cheese & yogurt

Both yogurt and cheese are made from milk that has been fermented. Plain, unflavored yogurt is the most useful type for cooking. You can buy full-fat or low-fat versions.

There are thousands of types of cheeses. You can cook with them in different ways — each recipe will tell you how.

This is Parmesan cheese. It can be grated or shaved.

Grated Parmesan

Parmesan shavings

Butter

Grating cheese

Scrape the cheese across the holes of a grater again and again. The recipe will tell you whether to use the large or small holes.

Shaving cheese

Sometimes recipes ask you to make shavings of hard cheese, such as Parmesan. Use a vegetable peeler to peel off strips of cheese.

Whipping cream

1 Pour the cream into a large bowl. Whip it with a whisk or electric mixer. Continue until the cream becomes thick.

2 To see if it's thick enough, lift up the whisk. The cream should stay in a floppy point. If you whisk for too long, the cream will become hard.

Softening butter

Butter is fairly hard when you get it out of the refrigerator. If a recipe says to use softened butter, take it out and leave it at room temperature for an hour before you start.

Pancakes

Ingredients:

1¾ cups self-rising (cake) flour

1 teaspoon of baking powder

2 teaspoons of sugar

1 large egg

1¼ cups milk or soy milk

1 tablespoon butter, margarine or
   dairy-free spread

vegetable oil, for frying

maple syrup or honey, for serving

Makes about 20

Pancakes are made by mixing milk with flour and egg to form a thick mixture called a batter. You fry spoonfuls of the batter in a pan until they set into pancakes.

    This recipe shows you how to cook small, puffy pancakes. They make a great breakfast for a special occasion.

Pancakes taste delicious
served with fresh fruit
and yogurt.

1 Sift the flour and baking powder into a large bowl. Add the sugar and stir it in.

2 Whisk the egg and milk together in a measuring cup. Take a large frying pan (preferably non-stick). Put in the butter, margarine or spread and heat gently until it has melted, then pour it into the measuring cup.

3 Pour the milk mixture into the flour. Beat it well with a whisk or a fork, to mix everything together and get rid of any lumps.

4 Put a tablespoon of oil in the frying pan. Put the pan on medium heat for 2-3 minutes. Drop a tablespoon of the batter into the pan, at one side.

Banana pancakes

Extra ingredient: 1 ripe banana.

Cut the banana into thin slices. Follow steps 1-3. Gently stir the banana slices into the batter. Follow steps 4-7.

Berry pancakes

Extra ingredients: ¾ cup fresh strawberries, raspberries or blueberries.

If you're using strawberries, pull out the green tops and cut the strawberries into thin slices. Follow steps 1-3. Gently stir the berries into the batter. Follow the rest of the steps.

5 Drop 2 or 3 more tablespoons of batter into other parts of the pan. Try to make sure the pancakes don't touch each other.

6 Cook for 3 minutes. You'll see small bubbles appear on top of the pancakes. Turn the pancakes over, then cook for 2-3 minutes more.

7 Put the pancakes on a warm plate and cover with a clean dishtowel. Heat a little more oil in the pan and make more pancakes, until all the batter is used up. Eat them warm, with the syrup or honey on top.

Buttermilk biscuits

Ingredients:

2½ cups all-purpose flour

1 teaspoon of baking soda

3 tablespoons of butter

¾ cup + 2 tablespoons buttermilk
   or plain yogurt

a little milk

You will also need a round cutter
   around 2½ inches across

Makes around 8

These biscuits are made with buttermilk, which is the liquid left over when milk is made into butter. When you mix the buttermilk with baking soda it creates tiny gas bubbles that make the biscuits light and airy.

You can also make bread in this way. It's called soda bread. You'll find instructions for making it on the opposite page.

1 Preheat the oven to 400°F. Then, use a paper towel to wipe a teaspoon of cooking oil over a cookie sheet.

2 Sift the flour and baking soda into a large bowl. This will help to mix the baking soda into the flour.

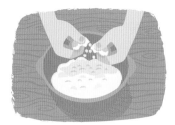

3 Cut the butter into small chunks. Add them to the flour. Rub them in with the tips of your fingers and thumbs until the mixture looks like small breadcrumbs (see page 149).

4 Put the buttermilk or yogurt in the bowl. Cut through the ingredients again and again with a blunt knife. Stop when they cling together in a lump.

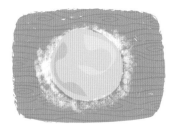

5 Pat the lump of dough into a smooth ball. Put it on a clean work surface lightly dusted with flour.

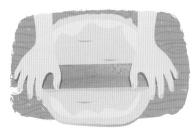

6 Roll out the dough until it is around twice as thick as your little finger (see page 149).

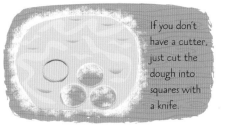

If you don't have a cutter, just cut the dough into squares with a knife.

7 Cut circles from the dough with the cutter. Squeeze the scraps into a ball and roll them out again. Cut more circles.

8 Put the biscuits on the cookie sheet, spacing them out well. Brush the tops with a little milk. Put the cookie sheet in the oven for 10 minutes.

9 The biscuits will rise and turn golden. When they are cooked, take the cookie sheet out of the oven and leave it for a few minutes. Then, put the biscuits on a wire rack to cool.

Soda bread

Follow steps 1-4, then, shape the dough into a flattened ball and put it on the cookie sheet. Cut a deep cross on the top of the dough. Bake for 20 minutes or until the soda bread is risen and sounds hollow when you tap it underneath. Cool on a wire rack.

Cheese biscuits

Extra ingredient: 1 cup coarse grated Cheddar or Monterey Jack cheese. Follow steps 1-3. Then, put all the cheese, except a small handful, in the bowl and mix it in. Follow steps 4-7. At step 8, sprinkle over the remaining cheese after brushing on the milk. Then, follow the rest of the steps.

Date & walnut biscuits

Extra ingredients: ⅓ cup diced dates (with the pits removed) and ½ cup walnut pieces. Follow steps 1-3. Put the dates and walnuts in the bowl and mix them in, then follow the rest of the steps. Contains nuts.

Biscuits taste best fresh, eaten on the day you make them.

Ice cream

Ingredients:

1 large, ripe banana

4 tablespoons powdered sugar

½ cup full-fat plain yogurt

⅔ cup heavy or whipping cream

a 1oz. package of store-bought meringue cookies or 1 cup crushed homemade meringues

You will also need a freezer-proof container with a tightly-fitting lid

Serves 4

You shouldn't re-freeze ice cream after it's softened. So eat it as soon as it's made.

Banana ice cream with chocolate sauce and nuts

Berry ice cream with berry sauce

Making your own ice cream is simple, but it takes a little time. This recipe is for banana ice cream, but there are recipes for other flavors, and ice cream sauces, on the page opposite. All the recipes use meringues: you could buy some, or use the recipe on page 60 to make them.

1 Put the banana in a bowl and mash it with a fork or a potato masher. Sift in the powdered sugar, add the yogurt and mix well.

2 Pour the cream into a large bowl. Whisk it until it is thick and makes points when you lift the whisk. Then, add the yogurt mixture to it.

3 Gently turn the mixture over with a spoon, to mix everything together. Then, pour it into the freezer-proof container and put on the lid.

4 Put the container in the freezer for 2 hours, or until the ice cream is mushy and half-frozen. Meanwhile, break the meringues into small pieces.

5 Take the ice cream out of the freezer. Mash it with a fork, to break up any ice crystals. Add the broken meringues and stir them in.

6 Put the ice cream back in the freezer for 4 hours, or until it is firm. Take it out around 15 minutes before you want to eat it, so that it can soften a little.

Berry ice cream

Replace the banana with 1¼ cups mixed fresh or frozen berries such as blackberries, blueberries and raspberries.

In step 1, use the berries instead of the banana. Follow steps 2-6.

Lemon ice cream

Replace the banana with ¼ cup lemon curd.

Put the lemon curd in a bowl, sift in the powdered sugar, add the yogurt and mix. Then, follow steps 2-6. You can use store-bought lemon curd, or make your own (see page 62).

Ice cream sauces

○ For chocolate sauce, put ⅔ cup heavy cream in a saucepan and heat gently until it steams. Add ½ cup semisweet chocolate chips and stir until smooth.

○ For berry sauce, put 4 handfuls of mixed berries and 4 tablespoons of powdered sugar in a bowl. Mash with a fork until smooth.

Chocolate pudding

Ingredients:

1 cup heavy cream

1 tablespoon of sugar

1 cup + 2 tablespoons semisweet chocolate chips

You will also need 4 small glasses, cups or dishes.

Serves 4

These little chocolate pudding cups are delicious and very easy to make. You just heat the cream and chocolate and pour it into four small cups to set — any small glasses, cups or dishes will do. There are instructions for lemon and raspberry pudding here, too.

Lemon pudding

You will need 1 lemon, 1 cup heavy cream and ¼ cup + 2 tablespoons sugar. Squeeze the juice from the lemon. Follow step 1. Turn down the heat. Let the mixture bubble gently for 3 minutes, stirring all the time. Turn off the heat. Stir in 3 tablespoons of the lemon juice, then follow steps 4-5.

1 Put the cream and sugar in a saucepan and put the pan on medium heat. Stir the mixture every now and then, until it starts to bubble.

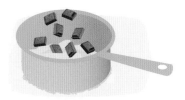

2 Turn off the heat. Put the chocolate chips in the saucepan with the hot cream.

3 Leave the chocolate to melt for around 2 minutes, then stir until the mixture is smooth.

4 Leave the mixture to cool in the pan for 10 minutes. Then, stir it and pour it into your dishes.

5 When the mixture is completely cold, put the dishes in the refrigerator for at least 4 hours.

To make chocolate curls like these, scrape a bar of chocolate with a vegetable peeler.

Raspberry pudding

You will need 2¼ cups fresh raspberries, 1 cup heavy cream and 2½ tablespoons of sugar. Put the raspberries in a bowl and mash them up with a fork. Follow step 1, then turn down the heat and let the mixture bubble gently for 3 minutes, stirring all the time. Turn off the heat. Stir in the raspberries, then follow steps 4-5.

You could decorate your cups with raspberries and mint leaves, if you like.

Quesadillas

Ingredients:

4oz. hard cheese such as
  Cheddar or Monterey Jack

2 green onions

2 tomatoes

4 soft flour or corn taco-sized tortillas
  (gluten-free types are available)

around 1 tablespoon of olive oil

You will also need 2 cookie sheets.

Serves 2

A quesadilla is a soft tortilla with a filling of melted cheese — the word means 'little cheesy thing' in Spanish. Quesadillas taste good with guacamole and a salad. But, if you're really hungry, you could add some cooked chicken or refried beans (see the page opposite).

1 Preheat the oven to 350°F. Grate the cheese on the big holes of a grater.

2 Trim off the root end and most of the dark green part from the green onions and throw them away. Cut the rest into small pieces. It's easiest to use scissors.

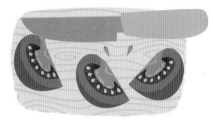

3 Put the tomatoes on a cutting board and cut them in half, then into quarters. Cut out the green cores. Then, chop the quarters into small pieces.

4 Brush a tortilla with a little of the oil. Put it oil-side down on a cookie sheet. Do the same with another tortilla.

5 Scatter around half the cheese over the tortillas, almost to the edges. Then, arrange the green onions and tomatoes over the cheese, and scatter the rest of the cheese on top.

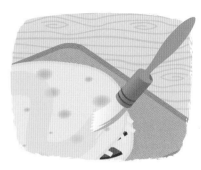

6 Top each pile with a second tortilla and brush the tops of the tortillas with the rest of the oil.

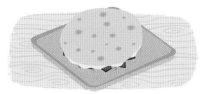

7 Put the cookie sheets in the oven and bake for 8-10 minutes, until the quesadillas are lightly browned.

8 Carefully lift the quesadillas onto plates, using a spatula. Then, cut each one into 4 wedges.

Chicken quesadillas

Extra ingredient: 1 cup cooked shredded chicken — leftover roast chicken is ideal, but you can also buy cooked chicken. Follow steps 1-4. At step 5, add the chicken before the final scattering of cheese. Then, follow the rest of the steps.

Bean quesadillas

To make quesadillas with refried beans, first cook the beans, following the instructions on the right. Then, follow steps 1-4 of the main recipe. Spread half the bean mixture over each tortilla before adding the other fillings, then follow steps 5-8.

Refried beans

You will need 1 small red onion, 1 clove of garlic, 2 tablespoons of vegetable oil and a 15oz. can of beans such as black beans or red kidney beans. Chop the onion finely. Crush the garlic. Put the oil, onion and garlic in a pan on medium heat. Cook for 10 minutes, stirring often. Meanwhile, drain the beans, pour them into a bowl and mash them until they are smooth. Put them in the pan, add 4 tablespoons of water, a pinch of salt and some pepper. Cook for 5 minutes, stirring often.

Feta cheese pies

Ingredients:

8oz. package of filo dough
   pastry sheets

½ stick (¼ cup) butter

1 large egg

8oz. package of ricotta cheese

7oz. package of feta cheese

6 sprigs of fresh dill weed

1 pinch of ground nutmeg (optional)

You will also need a pastry brush

Makes around 20

Feta is a white, crumbly cheese that's popular in Greece and Turkey. There, people make delicious pies from feta, eggs and herbs wrapped in a thin, crispy pastry known as filo. This recipe shows you how to make a simple version.

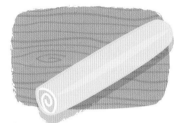 

1 Take the filo pastry out of the refrigerator. Leave it in its packaging for 20 minutes, to come to room temperature.

2 Put the butter in a small saucepan. Put the pan over low heat until the butter melts. Take the pan off the heat. Break the egg into a bowl, beat it with a fork, add the ricotta cheese and mix.

These pies can be eaten warm or cold.

3 Take the feta cheese out of its packaging and rinse it under cold water. Pat it dry with paper towels, then crumble it into the bowl with the eggs and ricotta.

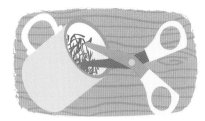

4 Break the hard stalks off the dill weed. Put the leaves in a cup and snip them into small pieces. Put the chopped dill weed in the bowl, add the nutmeg and some pepper and mix everything together.

Spinach & feta pies

Extra ingredient: ⅓ cup frozen spinach.

Defrost the spinach. Put it in a strainer over a bowl. Push down with the back of a spoon to squeeze out the water. Follow steps 1-2. At step 3, use just two-thirds of the feta. At step 4 add the spinach along with the dill weed. Follow steps 5-8.

5 Preheat the oven to 375°F. Unwrap and unroll the filo pastry. Cut it into strips each around 4 inches wide and 10 inches long. Cover the strips with a damp dishtowel so they don't dry out.

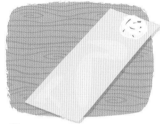

6 Brush some melted butter over two cookie sheets. Take a strip of pastry. Put a heaped teaspoonful of the filling at the top right-hand corner.

Big feta pie

Follow steps 1-4. Preheat the oven to 375°F. Brush the inside of an ovenproof dish with butter. Line it with 1 sheet of filo and brush it with butter. Add more sheets of filo, brushing each one with butter, until you have used one third of them. Spread on half the cheese mixture. Add half the remaining filo sheets, brushing each with butter. Add the rest of the cheese. Top with the rest of the filo, brushing each sheet with butter. Bake for 20-30 minutes until golden. Cut into slices.

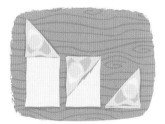

7 Fold the corner down to make a triangle. Keep folding the triangle down the length of the strip, to make a package. Put it on a cookie sheet. Make lots more.

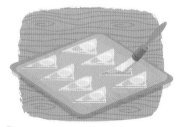

8 Brush the tops of the packages with melted butter. Bake for about 20 minutes, until they are golden and crisp. Leave them on the cookie sheets for a few minutes, then put them on a wire rack to cool.

If you don't have a pastry brush, you can spread on the butter using a paper towel.

Cheesecake

Ingredients:

6oz. graham crackers
  (or gluten-free cookies)

¾ stick (6 tablespoons) butter

1⅓ cups full-fat cream cheese

½ cup + 1 tablespoon sugar

2 large eggs

2 teaspoons of vanilla extract

You will also need an 8 inch spring
  form cake pan

Serves 6

This smooth vanilla cheesecake is made with cream cheese and baked in the oven until it sets firm. It's delicious on its own, but you could add a tangy fruit topping (see the page opposite). You'll also find a recipe for an easy lemon cheesecake. It's simpler to make because it sets in the refrigerator and doesn't need to be baked in the oven.

1 Take the cream cheese out of the refrigerator. Preheat the oven to 300°F. Wipe a little cooking oil over the inside of the pan with a paper towel.

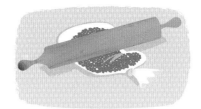

2 Put the crackers or cookies in a clean plastic bag. Seal the end with a rubber band. Roll a rolling pin over it to crush them into pieces the size of large breadcrumbs.

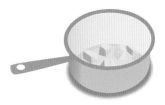

3 Put the butter in a saucepan and put it over low heat. When the butter has melted, turn off the heat.

4 Add the cracker or cookie crumbs to the butter and mix. Spoon the mixture into the pan. Press it flat with the back of a spoon. Put the pan in the refrigerator.

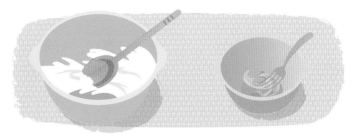

5 Meanwhile, put the cream cheese and sugar in a bowl and stir them together. Then, break the eggs into a small bowl, add the vanilla and mix them together with a fork.

6 Add a little egg to the cheese mixture and mix it in well. Do this again and again until the egg is all used up.

7 Pour the cheese mixture over the crumb base. Level the top with the back of a spoon. Bake for 30 minutes, then, turn off the oven and leave the cheesecake in for 30 minutes more.

8 Take the cheesecake out of the oven and leave it to cool on a wire rack. Then, refrigerate for at least 2 hours.

9 Remove the sides of the pan (see page 171). Then, slide the cheesecake onto a plate.

Berry topping

You will need around 1¼ cups mixed berries, 5 tablespoons of seedless raspberry jam and 1 tablespoon of lemon juice. Wash and dry the berries. Remove any stems from the strawberries. Pile the fruit onto the cheesecake. Mix the jam and lemon juice and brush the mixture over the fruit.

Easy lemon cheesecake

Replace the eggs and vanilla with ⅔ cup heavy or whipping cream and 2 large lemons.

Follow steps 1-4. Then, put just 1½ cups cream cheese in a bowl with the cream and sugar. Mix. Grate the zest from the lemons, then squeeze out the juice. Put the zest and juice in the bowl and mix. Spoon the mixture over the crumb base, level the top and refrigerate for at least 2 hours. Then, follow step 9.

About eggs

Eggs are used in all different types of dishes, from pasta and quiches to cakes and meringues. Here are some tips about cooking with eggs.

Big and small

You can buy big eggs from ducks or tiny eggs from quails, but most eggs are from chickens. Chicken eggs come in different sizes, too. All the recipes in this book use large chicken eggs.

Whites and yolks

The yellow part of an egg is the yolk. The clear part is the white. For some recipes you need both. For others, you need to separate them (see opposite).

Egg safety

Eating raw eggs can sometimes make people sick. Make sure food with eggs in it is cooked properly. And you shouldn't taste uncooked cake or cookie mix that contains egg, either.

Boiling eggs

Allow 1-2 eggs per person. Half fill a pan with water. Cook on medium heat until the water boils. Lower in the eggs. Adjust the heat so the water bubbles gently. It's difficult to give exact timings, but to hard-boil large eggs, cook for around 10-11 minutes. Cook for 1 less minute for medium eggs.

Chicken eggs can be white or brown.

This tiny, speckled egg was laid by a quail.

An egg yolk

Breaking an egg

1 Crack the shell by tapping it sharply on the edge of a bowl or cup.

2 Push your thumbs into the crack and pull the shell apart.

3 Let the yolk and white slide gently into the cup or bowl.

Beating an egg

Beat the yolk and white quickly with a fork, until they are mixed together.

Separating an egg

Break an egg and let the white and yolk slide onto a plate. Cover the yolk with a small cup, then hold the cup and tilt the plate, so the egg white slides off.

This is a foamy blob of whisked egg white.

Whisking egg whites

1 Beat the egg whites with a whisk or electric mixer. Continue until they become very thick and foamy.

2 Try lifting up the whisk or mixer — if the foam stays in a point you have whisked enough.

Scrambling eggs

1 Allow 1-2 eggs per person. Break them into a bowl. Add 1 tablespoon of milk per person, a pinch of salt and some pepper. Beat everything together with a fork.

2 Put a small chunk of butter in a pan. Put the pan on medium heat. When the butter melts, pour in the eggs. Stir for 2-3 minutes, until they set into fluffy clusters.

Frying eggs

1 Allow 1-2 eggs per person. Pour a tablespoon of oil into a frying pan. Put the pan on medium heat for 1 minute, then take it off.

2 Crack an egg, then hold it just above the pan and open the shell. Pour the egg into the pan, then put it back on the heat.

3 When the egg white starts to turn solid, spoon hot oil over the yolk. Fry the egg for 3-4 minutes.

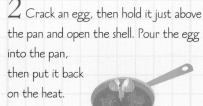

Quiche

Ingredients:

For the pastry:

1½ cups all-purpose flour

¾ stick (6 tablespoons) butter

For the filling:

1 large leek

1 tablespoon of olive or vegetable oil

5oz. sliced ham

1 pinch of ground nutmeg (optional)

4oz. hard cheese such as Cheddar, Monterey Jack or Gruyère

2 large eggs

⅔ cup milk

You will also need:

an 8 inch fluted tart pan with a loose base

a bag of dried peas or beans, for blind-baking

a large square of aluminum foil or parchment paper

Serves 4

A quiche is a pastry shell filled with a mixture of eggs and milk. In this recipe, the filling is flavored with cheese, ham and leeks. Before the filling is added, the pastry is 'blind baked' on its own. This helps the quiche to stay crisp underneath.

1 Put a cookie sheet in the oven and preheat the oven to 400°F. Make the pastry, following steps 1-7 on page 152. Then, line the tart pan with the pastry, following steps 1-3 on page 149.

2 Lay the foil or parchment over the pastry in the tart pan. Press it lightly on top of the pastry. Pour on a layer of dried beans. Lift out the hot cookie sheet and put the pan on it.

3 Bake for 10 minutes. Then, take it out and carefully lift off the hot beans and foil or parchment. Put the pan back in the oven for another 8-10 minutes, until the pastry is pale golden.

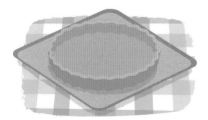 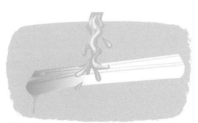 

4 Take the pan out of the oven. Put the hot cookie sheet back in the oven on its own. Reduce the oven temperature to 325°F. Next, make the filling.

5 Remove the root and most of the dark green top from the leek. Cut the leek in half lengthways. Wash it under cold water, fanning out the layers to wash out any dirt. Cut across the leek to make small slices.

6 Put the chopped leek in a saucepan with the oil. Cook on low heat for 5 minutes, with the lid on. Turn off the heat. Tear the ham into small pieces. Put them in the pan, add the nutmeg and some pepper and stir.

7 Grate the cheese using the large holes on a grater. Scatter half the cheese into the pastry shell. Put the leek and ham mixture on top, then scatter over the rest of the cheese.

8 Break the eggs into a measuring cup and beat them with a fork. Add the milk and mix it in. Carefully pour the milk mixture over the filling in the pie crust.

9 Lift the cookie sheet out of the oven, put the quiche on it and put it back in the oven. Bake for 30 minutes, or until the middle feels firm when you poke it with the point of a knife.

10 Leave the quiche to cool for 10 minutes. By then it will have become firm enough to cut into slices. You could eat it with some salad and bread.

Mushroom & onion

Replace the leeks and ham with 1¼ cups mushrooms and 1 onion.

Follow steps 1-4. Slice the mushrooms and onion. Put them in a saucepan with the oil. Cook on medium heat for 5 minutes. Add some pepper and the nutmeg. Follow step 7, using the mushrooms and onions instead of the ham and leeks. Follow steps 8-10.

Bacon & onion

Follow the instructions for the mushroom & onion quiche above, but replace the mushrooms with 6 slices of bacon, snipped into pieces.

Salmon & broccoli

Replace the leeks, ham and nutmeg with 7oz. broccoli and 4oz. smoked salmon. Follow steps 1-4. Cut up the broccoli. Boil for 5 minutes. Snip up the smoked salmon. Follow step 7, using the broccoli and salmon instead of the ham and leeks. Follow steps 8-10.

Quiche is equally delicious served warm or chilled.

Meringues

Ingredients:

For the meringues:

2 large eggs, at room temperature

7 tablespoons sugar

For the raspberry cream (optional):

1 cup fresh raspberries

¼ pint heavy or whipping cream

You will also need a large, shallow
   bowl that's very clean and dry

Makes around 20

Meringues are made of whisked egg whites and sugar, baked in the oven until the outsides are crisp, while the insides stay deliciously chewy. This recipe makes around 20 small meringues. Eat them just as they are, or sandwich pairs together with raspberry cream.

1 Preheat the oven to 225°F. Then, line two cookie sheets with parchment paper (see page 161).

2 Separate the eggs. Put the whites in the large, shallow bowl. You don't need the yolks for this recipe — you could use them to make the pasta on page 74.

3 Beat the egg whites very quickly with a whisk or electric mixer, until they become very thick and foamy. If the foam stays in a point, like this, when you lift up the whisk, you have whisked it enough.

4 Add a heaped teaspoonful of sugar to the foam and whisk until it is all mixed in. Keep on adding spoonfuls of sugar and whisking them in one at a time, until the sugar is all mixed in.

5 Put a heaped teaspoon of the mixture onto a cookie sheet (use another spoon to help). Continue until the mixture is used up. Leave gaps between them.

6 Bake for 40 minutes. Turn off the oven. Leave the meringues inside for 15 minutes. Then, lift them out and leave them to cool.

7 Meanwhile, make the raspberry cream. Rinse the raspberries in a strainer and shake them dry. Put them in a bowl and mash them until they are squashed and juicy.

White or golden

You can sometimes buy unrefined, golden sugar. If you make meringues using this, they will be a very pale golden color instead of white.

Passionfruit cream

Replace the raspberries with 3 ripe, wrinkly passionfruits. Follow steps 1-6. Cut the passionfruits in half and scoop out the seeds and juice with a spoon. Then, follow step 8. At step 9, add the passionfruit seeds and juice to the cream instead of the raspberries. Follow the rest of the step.

8 Pour the cream into a large bowl. Beat it with a whisk or electric mixer. Continue until it becomes thick. Try lifting up the whisk or mixer – if the cream stays in a floppy point you have whisked it enough.

9 Add the mashed raspberries to the cream and mix them in gently with a metal spoon. When the meringues are cold, spread the flat side of one with some raspberry cream. Then press the flat side of another meringue to the filling.

Lemon curd

Ingredients:

1 lemon

2 large eggs

⅓ cup sugar

½ stick (¼ cup) butter

You will also need a heatproof bowl that fits over a saucepan. The bottom of the bowl shouldn't touch the bottom of the saucepan.

Lemon curd is a delicious spread made with eggs, butter, sugar and lemons. It can be used to sandwich sponge cakes together (page 176), in pastry tarts, in ice cream (page 47), or just spread on some bread or toast.

1 Grate the zest from the outside of the lemon, using the small holes on a grater.

2 Cut the lemon in half and squeeze out all the juice.

3 Break the eggs into a heatproof bowl and beat them with a fork. Add the sugar and stir it in.

4 Put the zest and juice in the bowl with the egg and sugar. Cut the butter into chunks and put them in the bowl, too.

5 Fill a saucepan a quarter full of water. Put it on low heat, until the water is just bubbling. Wearing oven mitts, carefully put the bowl into the pan.

6 Stir the mixture with a wooden spoon. It will slowly start to thicken. Keep stirring all the time.

7 After about 20 minutes, check the back of the spoon. The mixture should coat it in an even layer.

8 Take the pan off the heat. Carefully take the bowl out of the pan. Leave the bowl until it is completely cold.

Redcurrant curd

Lemon curd

Lime curd

Simply replace the lemon with 2 limes. The finished lime curd will be a pale yellowish-green color, rather than a bright lime green.

Orange curd

Extra ingredient: 1 orange. Follow step 1. Grate the zest from the orange. Cut the orange and lemon in half and squeeze the juice from half of each. Then, follow steps 3-8.

Redcurrant curd

Extra ingredients: 7oz. fresh redcurrants.

Follow step 2. Wash the redcurrants and take them off their stalks. Put them in a pan with the lemon juice. Cook on medium heat for around 5 minutes, until the currants have split open. Pour the currants and juice into a strainer over a bowl. Use a spoon to push all the juice through. Follow steps 3-4, then add the redcurrant juice. Follow steps 5-8.

Lemon curd tart

Extra ingredients : 1½ cups all-purpose flour, ¾ stick (6 tablespoons) chilled butter and 2-3 tablespoons of cold water. You will also need an 8 inch pie pan.

Make the lemon curd. Then, make the pastry (see steps 1-7 on page 152). Line the pan (see page 149) and blind bake the pastry shell (see steps 1-3 on page 58). When the curd and pastry shell are cold, pour the curd into the shell. Refrigerate for 1 hour. Eat the tart chilled.

Omelette

SJ 30 June 2020

Ingredients:

2 large eggs

1 tablespoon butter, margarine or dairy-free spread

You will also need a medium-sized frying pan with a sloping edge.

Serves 1

Omelettes are like puffy pancakes made of eggs. They are quick and easy to make. You could add one of the fillings below, too.

1 Break the eggs into a bowl. Add 1 tablespoon of cold water, a pinch of salt and some pepper. Beat with a fork.

2 Put the butter in the pan. Put the pan on medium heat. When the butter foams, swirl it around the pan.

3 Pour in the eggs. Gently pull the edges into the middle with a fork. Then, tilt the pan to let any runny egg flow to the sides to cook.

4 When the top of the omelette has set but still looks creamy, carefully loosen the edges with a spatula. Fold the omelette over, then slide it onto a warmed plate.

Omelette fillings

Scatter any of these over your omelette before you fold it:

o ½ cup grated hard cheese, such as Cheddar

o a slice of ham, snipped into strips using scissors

o a handful of chopped fresh herbs

Pasta & potatoes

Find out how to make your own pasta, and create simple sauces for it, too.

Cook tasty potato dishes, from fries to potato salads.

About pasta

There are thousands of types of pasta, from thin spaghetti and flat lasagne to all kinds of noodles from countries such as China and Thailand. Here you can find out about different pastas, and how to cook them.

Dried or fresh

Pasta is made from flour and water, sometimes with added egg. A lot of pasta is then dried. You can also buy soft, 'fresh' pasta. Cook it in the same way as dried pasta; it just takes less time to cook.

Oriental noodles

Noodles have been made for centuries. Some types are made from wheat flour, but others are made from ground-up rice, beans or other ingredients.

How much to use

For a main meal, allow around ¾ cup dried pasta per person, depending on how hungry everyone is.

Allergy-free pasta

If you're cooking for people with allergies, you can buy pasta that's free of wheat, gluten, dairy, eggs and nuts. Follow the cooking instructions on the packaging.

Cooking spaghetti or other pasta

1 Half fill a large saucepan with water and put it on high heat. When the water boils, turn down the heat so it bubbles gently. Add a pinch of salt.

2 Add in the dried pasta, then give it a stir. For spaghetti, hold the spaghetti in a bunch at one end and put the other end into the water. As the spaghetti softens, press it into the water, then use a spoon to push in the ends and stir.

3 Boil for 8-12 minutes for dried pasta, a little less for fresh (check the packaging). When the pasta is cooked, drain it, then pour it back into the pan, add a sauce and stir.

When is it cooked?

Lift a piece of pasta out of the pan, rinse it in cold water and bite it. It should be tender but not soggy.

Lasagne is a classic baked pasta recipe.

Cooking noodles

Some types of noodles are partly cooked already. This means you can heat them up in just a few minutes. Check the cooking instructions on the packaging.

Baking pasta

Most store-bought lasagne pasta cooks in the oven, but some types need to be boiled first. Check the instructions on the packaging if you're not sure.

Simple pasta sauces

Ingredients:

1 large, leafy bunch of basil
 (around 2oz.)

1 small clove of garlic

1 lemon (optional)

½ cup pine nuts

6 tablespoons of olive oil

1½oz. Parmesan cheese
 (or ½ cup grated Parmesan)

To serve:

3 cups pasta (you could
 use allergy-free pasta)

Serves 4

These sauces are all quick and easy, and can be stirred into freshly cooked pasta. The main recipe is for basil pesto sauce, which contains nuts.

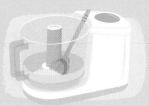

1 Pick the basil leaves off the stalks. Peel and crush the garlic. Cut the lemon in half and squeeze out the juice. Grate the Parmesan on the small holes of the grater.

2 If you're using a blender, put in the basil, garlic, lemon juice, pine nuts, oil, a pinch of salt and some pepper. Blend until you have a smooth paste. Stir in the Parmesan. Then, go to step 7.

3 If you're not using a blender, put the basil leaves in a mug and use scissors to snip them into tiny pieces. Put the snipped basil and the crushed garlic in a bowl.

4 Put the pine nuts in a clean plastic bag and secure the end with a rubber band. Roll a rolling pin over it to crush the pine nuts into small pieces. Put them in the bowl.

5 Put a tablespoon of oil in, too. Stir it in with a wooden spoon, pressing and crushing the mixture as you stir. Add the rest of the oil in the same way, a tablespoon at a time.

6 Put the lemon juice and grated Parmesan in the bowl and add a pinch of salt and some pepper. Mix everything together.

7 Next, cook your pasta (see page 67). To serve it, pour the pesto onto your drained pasta. Use two forks to lift and toss the pasta, until the pesto is mixed through.

Cheese & butter

You will need 3 cups pasta, ½ cup grated hard cheese such as Parmesan, Cheddar or Monterey Jack and a piece of butter around the size of a walnut.

Cook the pasta, drain it and put it back in the pan. Add the cheese, butter, a pinch of salt and some pepper. Mix.

Different pestos

You can make different flavors of pesto by replacing the pine nuts with the same amount of walnuts or almonds, or replacing the basil with flat-leaf parsley or fresh arugula leaves. Contains nuts.

Cream, garlic & cheese

You will need 3 cups pasta, 2 tablespoons butter, 1 clove of garlic, 1 cup light cream and ½ cup grated hard cheese such as Parmesan, Cheddar or Monterey Jack.

Put the pasta on to cook. Melt the butter in a pan on low heat. Crush in the garlic. Cook for around 20 seconds. Pour in the cream, whisking all the time. Add some pepper. Turn up the heat a little. Cook for 1 minute. Turn off the heat. Stir in the cheese until it melts. Mix into the pasta.

Chili, garlic & olive oil

You will need 3 cups pasta, 4 teaspoons of olive oil, 1 clove of garlic and 1 pinch of crushed red pepper.

Put the pasta on to cook. When it is almost cooked, put the olive oil in a pan on medium heat. Crush in the garlic. Add the crushed red pepper. Cook for 1 minute. Drain the pasta, put it back in the pan, pour on the sauce and mix.

Pasta soup

Ingredients:

4 slices of smoked sliced bacon

1 leek or onion

2 carrots

1 vegetable bouillon cube

2½ tablespoons of tomato paste or
    sun-dried tomato paste

1 tablespoon of olive oil

1 clove of garlic

1 teaspoon of Italian herb blend

⅓ cup small dried pasta shapes such as
    orzo (you could use allergy-free pasta)

6 sprigs of fresh parsley

grated Parmesan cheese, to
    serve (optional)

Serves 4

This recipe is based on an Italian pasta soup called minestrone, which can be made with lots of different combinations of vegetables. So, for example, you could replace the carrots with zucchini, or the leeks with finely chopped cabbage. There's also a meat-free version on the page opposite.

1 Using clean kitchen scissors, snip the bacon into strips around ½ inch wide.

2 Cut the leek in half lengthways. Cut off most of the dark green leaves and the roots. Wash the leek halves under cold water. Then, cut the leek into thin slices. If you're using an onion, cut it into small pieces.

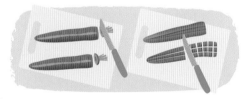

3 Scrub the carrots (or peel them if they are really muddy). Cut off the tops and throw them away, then cut the carrots into small cubes around ½ inch wide.

4 Put the bouillon cube in a heat-proof measuring cup and pour in 2½ cups of boiling water. Add the tomato paste. Stir until the cube has dissolved.

5 Heat the oil in a saucepan. Add the bacon and cook for 2 minutes, stirring often, until it is beginning to turn golden.

6 Crush in the garlic, add the leek and cook for 2 minutes, stirring, until it is beginning to soften. Stir in the carrots.

Meat-free pasta soup

Extra ingredient: a 15oz. can of beans such as cannellini beans, white kidney beans or chickpeas.

Follow steps 2-7, leaving out the bacon. Then, open the can of beans and pour the contents into a strainer. Rinse the beans under cold running water to remove all the liquid, then shake them dry and put them in the pan. Then, follow steps 8 and 9.

7 Pour the bouillon into the pan. Add 2½ cups boiling water, the herbs and some pepper. Bring the soup to a boil, then put a lid on the pan, leaving a small gap. Let it bubble gently for 15 minutes.

8 Put the pasta in the pan, put the lid back on and cook for 10 more minutes. While the soup is cooking, break the stalks off the parsley. Put the leaves in a cup and snip them into small pieces.

9 Turn off the heat and stir in the parsley leaves. Ladle the soup into 4 bowls and sprinkle some grated Parmesan on top of each.

71

Lasagne

Ingredients:

For the Bolognese sauce:

1 onion

2½ tablespoons of olive oil

1 clove of garlic

½ teaspoon of dried oregano

1lb. lean ground beef

1 beef or vegetable bouillon cube

a 15oz. can of diced
  tomatoes

4 tablespoons of tomato paste

2 teaspoons of balsamic vinegar

5 sprigs of fresh basil (optional)

For the white sauce:

2½ cups milk

1 slice of onion

1 bay leaf

¼ cup (½ stick) butter

½ cup all-purpose flour

You will also need:

6oz. oven-ready lasagne
  (you could use allergy-free lasagne)

¼ cup grated Parmesan cheese

a large ovenproof pan

Serves 4

It takes quite a long time to make lasagne, but the results are so delicious, it's worth it. You could eat your lasagne with one of the salads on pages 28-29.

1 Make the Bolognese sauce following the instructions on page 91. While the Bolognese is cooking, start making the white sauce.

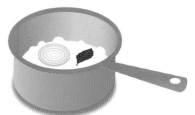

2 Pour the milk into a large saucepan. Add the slice of onion, the bay leaf and some pepper. Cook on medium heat.

3 When the milk starts to bubble, turn down the heat so it bubbles very gently. Leave for 5 minutes. Then, pour the milk into a strainer over a bowl. Throw away the onion and bay leaf.

4 Put the butter in the pan. Cook on low heat, until the butter melts. Then, take the pan off the heat.

5 Put a spoonful of flour in the pan and stir it in well. Add the rest of the flour a spoonful at a time, stirring well each time.

6 Add a little milk. Stir it in quickly to make a smooth paste, squashing any lumps against the side of the pan. Add more milk in the same way, a little at a time, until it is all mixed in.

Continue stirring all the time.

7 Put the pan over medium heat. When the mixture boils, cook it for 1 minute, then take the pan off the heat. Preheat the oven to 350°F.

8 Rub a little butter over the inside of the ovenproof pan. Spoon in one third of the Bolognese. Spoon a quarter of the white sauce over it. Top with a layer of lasagne sheets.

9 Make two more layers of Bolognese, white sauce and lasagne sheets in the same way. Cover the final lasagne sheets with the remaining white sauce.

10 Sprinkle the Parmesan cheese over the top of the lasagne. Bake for 35-45 minutes, or until the top is browned and bubbling.

11 Push a sharp knife into the lasagne. The knife should slide in easily. If it doesn't, bake for another 5-10 minutes and test again. Leave to cool for 5 minutes before eating.

Homemade pasta

Ingredients:

2 cups all-purpose flour or '00' pasta flour

1/2 teaspoon of salt

3 large eggs

1 tablespoon of olive oil

1 tablespoon of cold water

Serves 4

Pasta is very satisfying to make, and it's easy too. You don't need a pasta machine — just use a rolling pin and then shape it by hand. Use pasta flour, often called '00' flour, if you can find it, but all-purpose flour is fine too.

1 Put the flour and salt in a large bowl. Then, make a hollow in the middle.

You don't need the white — save it for another recipe such as meringues (page 60).

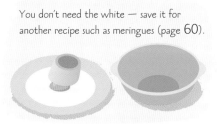

2 Break open one egg and separate the yolk from the white (see page 57). Pour the yolk into the hollow in the flour.

3 Break another egg, then pour it all into the hollow. Do the same with the last egg. Put the oil and water in the hollow, too.

4 Use a fork to mix the eggs together in the hollow. Then, start to mix in some flour from the edges of the hollow. Continue until you have mixed in all the flour and you have a ball of dough.

5 Sprinkle a little flour over a clean work surface. Put the dough on the surface and knead it for around 5 minutes until it is very smooth and springy (see page 135).

6 Wrap the dough in plastic food wrap. Put it in the refrigerator for 30 minutes. Meanwhile, you could make a sauce for your pasta (see pages 32, 68 or 91).

7 Unwrap the dough and put it back on the floury surface. Cut it into 3 pieces. Roll it out, following the instructions on page 149. Keep on rolling until the dough is around 10 inches wide and 12 inches long.

8 Shape your sheet of pasta following the instructions below. Roll out and shape the other pieces of the dough in the same way. Sprinkle a little flour over two clean dishtowels and spread out all your pasta shapes to dry for 5 minutes. Then, cook them by following the instructions on page 67 for boiled pasta, or page 72 for baked pasta.

Lasagne

Use a knife to cut the dough into 6 wide rectangles. Lasagne sheets are used in pasta bakes, which are also called lasagne (see page 72).

Pappardelle

Cut the pasta into long strips around 1 inch wide. These shapes are known as 'pappardelle'. They are good for eating with meaty sauces such as Bolognese (see page 91).

Stracci

Cut across the pasta diagonally one way, then the other, to make diamonds. They are also good with meaty sauces.

Farfalle

Cut the pasta into wide strips, like pappardelle, then into pieces around 1½ inches long. Pinch each piece in the middle. They are best eaten with creamy or tomato sauces (see page 32).

Thai-style noodles

Ingredients:

1 teaspoon of cornstarch

1 teaspoon of sesame oil (for those
   with nut allergies, use vegetable oil)

7oz. raw large shrimp

9oz. package of stir-fry rice noodles

½ cup salted peanuts (optional)

1 lime

1 tablespoon of light brown sugar

2 tablespoons of Thai fish sauce

6 green onions

1 clove of garlic

2 tablespoons of sunflower oil

1 pinch of crushed red pepper

3 cups bean sprouts

8-10 sprigs of cilantro leaves

Serves 4

This noodle dish comes from Thailand and is often called Pad Thai. It is made with rice noodles, shrimp, bean sprouts and peanuts, flavored with Thai fish sauce (also known as nam pla). You could leave out the peanuts if you prefer.

Eggy noodles

Leave out the shrimp. Skip step 1. Break 3 eggs into a bowl. Beat with a fork. Follow step 2. In step 3, replace the fish sauce with 2 teaspoons of soy sauce (or gluten-free tamari). Follow steps 4-5, skip step 6 and follow steps 7-9. Pour in the eggs. Leave for 1 minute, then stir to break up the egg. Follow step 10.

1 Put the cornstarch and sesame oil in a bowl. Put the shrimp in too and stir to coat them in the mixture. Put aside while preparing the other ingredients.

2 Put the noodles in a large heatproof bowl, pour boiling water over them and leave them for 4 minutes. Then, drain them in a strainer or colander.

3 Put the peanuts on a board and chop them roughly. Squeeze the juice from the lime and put it in a measuring cup. Put the sugar and fish sauce in the cup too, and stir.

4 Trim the roots and most of the dark green part from the green onions and throw them away. Then, chop the rest into ½ inch slices. Peel the papery skin off the garlic.

5 Put 1 tablespoon of the vegetable oil in a large frying pan or wok. Put the pan over high heat for a minute or two.

6 Put the shrimp in the pan. Keep stirring them around the pan briskly for around 1 minute, or until they have turned pink all over. Then, lift them out and put them on a plate.

7 Put the second tablespoon of oil in the pan. Leave it to heat up the oil for a few seconds. Add the green onions and crushed red pepper. Cook for 1 minute, stirring briskly.

8 Put the bean sprouts in the pan and crush in the garlic. Cook for 2 minutes, stirring briskly all the time, until the bean sprouts have softened slightly.

9 Put the shrimp back in the pan. Add the noodles and half the chopped peanuts. Pour over the lime juice mixture and cook for 1-2 minutes, stirring gently, until everything is steaming and hot.

10 To serve, sprinkle on the rest of the chopped peanuts and the cilantro leaves. If you prefer, you could chop the cilantro leaves first. Drizzle over some sweet and sour sauce too, if you like.

About potatoes

New potatoes

These knobbly potatoes are a type of new potato.

New potatoes

Small potatoes are often called new potatoes, because they're dug up sooner than large potatoes. They are good for boiling and for salads. They also have thin skin, so they are often cooked with their skins on.

A type of sweet potato with a white inside.

These potatoes have purplish skins but white insides.

Large potatoes

Large potatoes grow bigger than new potatoes, because they're left in the ground for longer. Some have fluffy insides, so they're good for mashing and making fries. Others are firmer, which makes them better for boiling.

Sweet potatoes

Sweet potatoes are distantly related to ordinary potatoes. They can be cooked like other potatoes, but the cooking times may vary.

Skin or no skin?

Most of the vitamins in potatoes are just under the skin, so it's healthier (and easier) to eat them with their skins on. But, if you can't wash all the mud off your potatoes, you might want to peel them.

Peeled potato

Scrubbing potatoes

Use a stiff brush to scrub potatoes in cold water. Try to get all the dirt off before you cook them.

Peeling potatoes

Hold the potato and scrape it again and again with a vegetable peeler until you have removed all the skin.

Boiling potatoes

1 Leave small potatoes whole. Cut large potatoes into similar-sized pieces. Put them in a saucepan. Cover with cold water. Add a pinch of salt.

2 Cook on medium heat. When the water boils, turn the heat down so it bubbles gently. Put a lid on, leaving a small gap. Cook for 15-20 minutes. Poke a knife into a potato. If it feels tender, the potatoes are cooked.

3 Pour the potatoes and water into a colander over the sink, to drain. To serve them hot, as a side dish, top with a little butter. For cold dishes such as potato salads, leave them in the colander to cool.

Mashing potatoes

1 If you want a really smooth mash, peel the potatoes. Cut them into bite-sized pieces.

2 Boil the potatoes following the instructions above. Then, drain them and pour them back in the pan.

3 Add the amount of butter the recipe says, and a pinch of salt. Use a potato masher to mash until there are no lumps left.

See page 84 for a potato-topped fish casserole.

Baked potatoes

Ingredients:

4 big potatoes, or 8 small ones

a little butter, margarine
   or dairy-free spread

other toppings and fillings —
   see the suggestions below

Serves 4

This recipe works
equally well for
potatoes and for
sweet potatoes.

Plain baked potatoes go well with main dishes such as kebabs or ribs (pages 96 and 102). But, if you add a topping, you can turn a baked potato into a meal in itself. You'll find suggestions for lots of toppings below.

1 Preheat the oven to 350°F. Use a fork to prick lots of holes all over the potatoes. Then, put them on a cookie sheet.

2 Put the cookie sheet in the oven and bake for 1 hour. Then, take it out carefully, wearing oven mitts.

Cheesy toppings

To top 4 potatoes, you will need around 1½ cups grated hard cheese such as Cheddar or Monterey Jack. Simply pile the cheese onto the baked potatoes. You could use 2 tablespoons of soft cheese instead, or add 2 tablespoons of warmed baked beans from a can (or see page 130 for a recipe) or tomato salsa (see page 27) to each potato.

3 Still wearing oven mitts, squeeze the potatoes gently. If they feel soft, they're ready. If not, bake them for 15 minutes more.

4 When the potatoes are ready, cut a cross in the top of each one. Put a small blob of butter or spread on top of each cross. Add a filling too, if you like.

Chicken toppings

To top 4 potatoes, you will need a can of cooked chicken (around 12oz.) and 5 tablespoons of mayonnaise.
Drain the chicken. Put it in a bowl, add the mayonnaise and some black pepper and mix. You could add 2 chopped green onions and 2 tablespoons of corn kernels, too.

Creamy toppings

To top 4 potatoes, you will need a small bunch of fresh chives, ²⁄₃ cup sour cream and ²⁄₃ cup plain yogurt.
Snip the chives into small pieces. Put them in a bowl, add the sour cream and yogurt, mix, then spoon it over the potatoes. You could also add some cooked bacon, snipped into strips.

Other toppings

Many of the recipes in this book, such as coleslaw (page 29) and guacamole (page 27), make great baked potato toppings. Just put a couple of tablespoons on top of each potato. You could also use warmed ratatouille (page 36), chili, bean chili or Bolognese sauce (pages 90-91).

Potato salads

Ingredients:

1½lbs. small new potatoes

½ red onion

For the dressing

1 tablespoon of white wine vinegar

1 tablespoon of mayonnaise (optional)

1 teaspoon of Dijon mustard

1 large sprig of fresh dill weed (optional)

Serves 4

Boiled new potatoes make delicious salads that can be eaten warm or cold. The main recipe here is for a simple potato salad, but there are ideas for others, too.

1 Scrub the potatoes. Cut up any big ones into chunks the same size as the smaller potatoes. Put them in a saucepan. Cover them with cold water. Add a pinch of salt

Tuna potato salad

You will need 12oz. small new potatoes, 8oz. thin string beans, 1 head butter lettuce, ½ red onion, 6 ripe cherry tomatoes, a 5oz. can of tuna in oil, and a dressing (see page 29).

Follow step 1. At step 2, put the potatoes on to cook, then snip the ends off the beans. Add the beans to the saucepan after the potatoes have been cooking for 10 minutes and complete the rest of the step. Follow step 3. Then, break the leaves off the lettuce. Wash and dry the leaves and break them into pieces. Halve the cherry tomatoes. Drain the tuna. Put all the salad ingredients in a bowl, add the dressing and mix.

You could add some black olives and canned chicken instead of the tuna.

Lemon mayo potato salad

You will need 1½lbs. small new potatoes, 4 green onions, ½ lemon, 3½ tablespoons of mayonnaise and 5 tablespoons of plain yogurt.

Follow steps 1-2. Drain the potatoes. Trim the green onions and snip them into small pieces. Squeeze the juice from the lemon. Mix the mayonnaise, yogurt and lemon juice in a large bowl. Add the potatoes and green onions and mix gently.

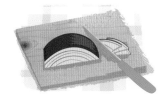

2 Cook on medium heat. When the water boils, turn the heat down so the water boils gently. Put on a lid, leaving a small gap, and cook for 15-20 minutes.

3 Meanwhile, cut the half onion into very thin slices and cut the slices into small pieces. When the potatoes are cooked, drain them in a colander over the sink.

4 To make the dressing, put the vinegar, mayonnaise and mustard in a cup. Mix very well with a fork. Then, put the dill weed in a mug and snip into small pieces using scissors.

5 Put the potatoes and onion in a large bowl. Pour the dressing on, scatter on the dill weed and mix everything together gently, to coat the salad evenly in the dressing.

Sweet potato salads

You could make a salad using 1½lbs. sweet potatoes. Peel them and cut them into chunks around ¾ inch across. Put them in a saucepan and cover them with cold water. Cook on medium heat. Follow step 2, but cook for just 10 minutes, or until the potatoes are tender. Then drain, cool and add your other salad ingredients, plus a dressing.

This sweet potato salad was made with red onion and salami.

Pesto potato salad

You will need 1½lbs. new potatoes, 4 tablespoons of basil pesto and a block of Parmesan cheese. Follow steps 1-2. Drain and cool the cooked potatoes. Put them in a bowl, pour over the pesto and mix. Shave the Parmesan (see page 41) and scatter it on top. (Pesto contains nuts.)

You could use store-bought pesto, or make your own (see page 68).

Fish & potato casserole

Ingredients:

½ vegetable bouillon cube

¾ cup frozen peas (optional)

1½lbs. potatoes

½ lemon

1lb. fillets of firm fish, such as salmon
 or flounder, defrosted if frozen

1 bay leaf

1¼ cups milk

1 stick (½ cup) butter

6 green onions or 1 small leek

½ cup all-purpose flour

½ cup cooked shelled
 shrimp (optional)

¼ cup grated hard cheese such as
 Cheddar or Monterey Jack (optional)

You will also need:

a large ovenproof pan

a potato masher

Serves 4

This recipe shows how to make a fish casserole with a crispy mashed potato topping. There's also a quicker version at the bottom of the page opposite.

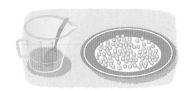

1 Put the half bouillon cube in a heatproof measuring cup. Add ⅔ cup boiling water. Stir until the cube has dissolved. Spread the peas on a plate to defrost.

2 Scrub the potatoes (or peel them if they are very muddy) and cut them into small chunks. Squeeze the juice from the lemon.

3 Put the fish and bay leaf in a saucepan. Pour in the bouillon and milk. Add some pepper. Cook on medium heat. When it starts to boil, turn down the heat so it bubbles very gently.

4 Cook for 5 minutes, then turn off the heat. Lift the fish out onto a plate. Pour the milky bouillon into a measuring cup. When it cools, take out the bay leaf.

5 Put the potatoes in the pan. Cover them with cold water. Put the pan on medium heat. When the water boils, turn down the heat so it bubbles gently. Cook for 15 minutes.

6 While the potatoes cook, use a fork to break the fish into big flakes. Remove any bones or skin. Then, cut the roots and green ends off the green onions or leek and cut the pale green and white parts into thin slices.

7 When the potatoes are soft, drain them and pour them back into the pan. Add half the butter and some pepper. Mash them until they are smooth.

8 Put the remaining butter in another large saucepan. Put it on low heat. When the butter melts, add the green onions or leeks. Cook for 5 minutes, stirring often.

Continue stirring all the time.

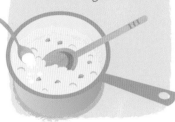

9 Add a spoonful of flour and stir it in. Continue adding more flour in the same way, until it is used up. Cook the mixture for 1 minute. Take the pan off the heat.

Continue stirring now, too.

10 Add a little fishy milk and stir it in. Add more milk in the same way, until it is used up. Put the pan on medium heat. When the mixture boils, leave it for 1 minute.

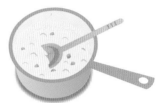

11 Put the fish, shrimp, peas and lemon juice in the pan, Stir them in gently. Cook the mixture for 3 minutes, then turn off the heat. Turn the broiler to medium.

12 Spoon the fish mixture into your dish, spread the mashed potatoes on top and scatter over the cheese. Broil for 5 minutes, until the cheese melts and the potatoes are crispy.

Easy fish & potato casserole

You will need 2 lbs. potatoes, 1 tablespoon butter, 6 green onions, 1 lb. skinless fillets of firm fish (such as salmon or flounder), ¾ cup raw, shelled large shrimp, ¾ cup frozen peas (optional) and 1 cup full-fat cream cheese or mascarpone cheese.

Preheat the oven to 350°F. Scrub or peel the potatoes. Cut them up. Follow step 5, then step 7, but put in all the butter. Prepare the green onions as in step 6. Cut the fish into bite-sized chunks. Put the green onions, fish, shrimp, peas and cheese in an ovenproof pan with a pinch of salt and some pepper. Mix. Spread on the mashed potatoes. Bake for 25 minutes. Make sure the fish is cooked all the way through and the shrimp is pink.

85

Homemade oven fries

Ingredients:

1½ lbs. large potatoes, preferably
ones suitable for baking,
such as russet potatoes

2½ tablespoons of cooking oil

a seasoning, such as 1 pinch of
crushed red pepper, 1 teaspoon of
ground paprika, ½ teaspoon of Italian
herb seasoning or 1 clove of garlic

Serves 4

These oven-baked French fries don't use much oil, so they're healthier than regular French fries, and easier to cook, too.

1 Preheat the oven to 400°F.

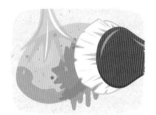

2 Scrub the potatoes, or peel them if they are very muddy.

3 Cut the potatoes into slices around ¾ inch wide, then cut them into French fry shapes.

4 Put the oil on a cookie sheet. Add the fries. Scatter on any seasonings, or peel and crush the clove of garlic over the fries.

5 Mix the fries around, to coat them in the oil and seasonings. Then, put the cookie sheet in the oven. Cook for 20 minutes.

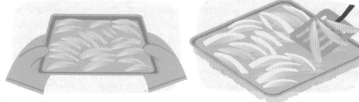

6 Take the cookie sheet out and turn the fries over. Cook for another 20 minutes or so, checking regularly to see how they are cooking. They're done when they're soft in the middle. They may take longer if there's something else in the oven as well.

Meat & fish

Make a beef stew, complete
with vegetables and dumplings,
cooked in one pan.

As well as the recipes in this section, you'll also find recipes for meatballs on
page 33, lamb tagine on page 128 and fish & potato casserole on page 84.

About meat

Here are some useful tips for preparing and cooking meat, including the easiest way to cook it and some basic meat safety advice.

Meat & poultry

Meat such as pork, beef and lamb is sold in pieces or ground. Meat from birds, such as chickens, ducks and turkeys, is known as poultry. You can buy poultry whole, in pieces, or, sometimes, ground.

Herbs & spices

Thyme and rosemary taste good with chicken, while mint and cilantro go well with lamb. Bay leaves are good with almost any kind of meat, while crushed red pepper gives a spicy kick to anything and everything meaty. There aren't any fixed rules — just experiment and see which flavors you prefer together.

Cured meat

Some types of meat, such as ham, bacon, corned beef and pastrami, have been cured first — this means salted, smoked or dried. Some cured meats need to be cooked before you eat them, but others are safe to eat just as they are.

Meat safety

Raw meat, especially chicken, can contain harmful bacteria. Wash your hands, and any knives and cutting boards, as soon as you've finished handling it.

Fruits, such as these figs, can go well with meat.

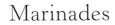

Cutting off fat

Use a sharp knife to trim any white, fatty pieces from your meat before you start cooking.

Marinades

Before you cook meat you can soak it in a liquid called a marinade, made from ingredients such as oil, lemon juice and herbs or spices. This helps to soften the meat and will add flavor, too.

Pan-frying meat

1 To pan-fry meat such as steak or chicken breasts, put a non-stick frying pan on high heat for a minute.

2 Pour in half a tablespoon of olive oil for each piece of meat. Tip the pan to coat it with the oil. Add the pieces of meat carefully.

3 For a thin-cut steak, cook for 2-4 minutes, then turn and cook the other side. For chicken, cook for around 6 minutes per side; make sure it is cooked through.

Broiling meat

1 To broil meat such as bacon, steak or chicken breasts, turn the broiler to medium temperature and leave it to heat up. Arrange the meat in the broiler pan.

2 For bacon, broil for 2-3 minutes per side, until it looks crispy. For steak, broil for around 4-6 minutes per side. For chicken, cook for around 8 minutes per side; make sure it is cooked through.

When is it cooked?

To check if meat such as pork is cooked, cut all the way through a piece. It should look cooked and the same color all the way through.

Properly cooked chicken should be white and firm all through, too. If there's any pink meat or juices, cook the chicken for longer.

Chili

Ingredients:

1 onion

1 red bell pepper

2 tablespoons of olive oil

1 clove of garlic

2 large pinches of crushed red pepper

½ teaspoon of dried oregano

1 teaspoon of ground cumin

1lb. lean ground beef

1 beef or vegetable bouillon cube

a 14oz. can of diced tomatoes

3½ tablespoons of tomato paste

a 15oz. can of red kidney beans

1 teaspoon of unsweetened cocoa powder
   or 2 squares of plain chocolate

a few sprigs of fresh cilantro (optional)

⅔ cup plain yogurt (optional)

Serves 4

This chili goes well with rice, nachos (page 132) or soft flour tortillas and guacamole (page 27). Or you can adapt the recipe to make bean chili or Bolognese — see opposite.

1 Peel the onion and cut off the ends. Cut the onion in half, cut the halves into slices and the slices into small pieces.

2 Cut the top off the bell pepper. Cut the bell pepper in half. Remove the seeds and white pith. Cut the bell pepper into bite-sized pieces.

3 Put the oil in a large saucepan and add the bell pepper and onion. Cook on medium heat for 5 minutes, stirring often. Crush and add the garlic.

4 Add the red pepper, oregano and cumin. Cook for 1 minute, stirring. Add the beef and cook for about 10 minutes, stirring, until it's brown all over. Break up any lumps with the spoon.

5 Put the bouillon cube in a heatproof measuring cup. Add 1¼ cups boiling water and stir until the cube dissolves.

6 Add the bouillon, tomatoes and tomato paste. Heat until the mixture boils, then turn down the heat so it just bubbles. Put a lid on the pan, leaving a small gap. Cook for 15 minutes.

7 Pour the red kidney beans into a strainer or colander and rinse well. Shake to get rid of any excess water. Put the beans in the pan, then stir in the cocoa powder or chocolate. Simmer without a lid for another 15 minutes.

8 While the chili is cooking, pick the leaves off the cilantro stalks. Put the leaves in a mug and snip them into small pieces using kitchen scissors.

9 Put the chopped herbs in a small bowl with the yogurt and mix them together. Add a dollop of the yogurt and cilantro to the top of your chili.

Bean chili

For a meat-free chili, follow steps 1-3. At step 4 leave out the beef. Follow step 5, using a vegetable bouillon cube. Follow step 6. At step 7, add an extra 15oz can of kidney beans or mixed beans, too. Follow steps 8-9.

Bolognese sauce

Replace the red bell pepper, crushed red pepper, cumin, kidney beans, cocoa or chocolate, yogurt and cilantro with 2 teaspoons of balsamic vinegar and 5 sprigs of fresh basil. Follow step 1. Follow step 3 to cook the onion and garlic, leaving out the bell pepper. At step 4, leave out the red pepper and cumin but add the vinegar. Follow steps 5 and 6. Cook the Bolognese for an extra 15 minutes, take off the lid and cook for another 20 minutes. When it's cooked, tear the basil leaves into small strips and stir them in. Eat with boiled spaghetti and grated Parmesan cheese.

Burgers

Ingredients:

2 slices of bread (see below for a gluten-free option)

1 tablespoon of balsamic vinegar

1 pinch of crushed red pepper (optional)

2 sprigs of fresh parsley or cilantro (optional)

1 onion

1lb. lean ground beef

Serves 4

Gluten-free burgers

To make this recipe gluten- and wheat-free, just use gluten-free bread instead of ordinary bread.

Turkey or pork burgers

Instead of beef, you could use the same amount of ground turkey or pork. Turkey burgers go well with garlic — crush 1 clove into the bowl at step 3. And for pork burgers, you could add a teaspoon of mustard to the mixture at step 2, instead of the red pepper.

Homemade burgers are easy to cook, and you can make them from any ground meat you like. The main recipe shows you how to make 4 hamburger patties. You can use the same ingredients to make meatballs (page 33).

1 Preheat the oven to 400°F. Then, put a teaspoon of cooking oil on a cookie sheet. Wipe the oil over the cookie sheet with a paper towel.

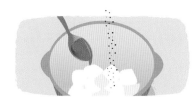

2 Trim the crusts off the bread. Tear the bread into small pieces. Put them in a large mixing bowl. Sprinkle on 4 tablespoons of cold water, the balsamic vinegar and red pepper.

3 Pick the leaves off the cilantro or parsley. Put them in a cup and snip them into tiny pieces using kitchen scissors. Put them in the bowl, too. Mix everything together.

4 Peel the onion and cut off the ends. Cut the onion in half, cut the halves into thin slices and the slices into tiny pieces.

5 Use a fork to mash the bread and the other ingredients in the bowl, until you have a fairly smooth mixture.

6 Put the chopped onion in the bowl, along with the beef, a pinch of salt and some pepper. Use your hands to mix and squash all the ingredients together.

7 Divide the mixture into four pieces. Pat each piece into a circle around 1/2 inch thick. Then, put the burgers on the greased cookie sheet.

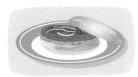

8 Cook the burgers in the oven for 10 minutes. Then, lift out the cookie sheet, wearing oven mitts. Turn them over and cook for another 10 minutes.

9 Push a knife into a burger, then press down on it. The juices that run out should be clear, not pink. If they are pink, cook for another 5-10 minutes.

10 You could serve your burger on a burger bun, with some lettuce and slices of tomato and onion, or some homemade guacamole or tomato salsa (page 27).

Chicken casserole

Ingredients:

8 skin-on chicken thighs or drumsticks, or 4 small, skin-on chicken breasts

2½ tablespoons of cooking oil, such as sunflower or olive oil

½ teaspoon of dried rosemary or a small sprig of fresh rosemary

1 onion

1 red or yellow bell pepper

1 clove of garlic

½ chicken or vegetable bouillon cube

1 lemon

a 14oz. can of diced tomatoes

You will also need a wide, shallow oven-proof casserole dish. If you don't have one, you could use a roasting pan.

Serves 4

Adding olives

At step 10, take the casserole out of the oven after it has been cooking for 20 minutes. Add around 12 black olives with the pits removed. Return the casserole to the oven for 10 more minutes.

Casserole is a French word, meaning a type of oven-proof pan. Food cooked in a casserole is also called a casserole. This chicken casserole can be eaten with bread, rice, pasta or potatoes.

1 Arrange the shelves in your oven so there's a shelf high up where your casserole fits. Then, preheat the oven to 400°F.

2 Arrange the chicken in the casserole so that the pieces are skin-side up, and don't overlap. Pour 1 tablespoon of the oil over the chicken, then spread it over the skin with your hands. Wash your hands well.

3 Scatter the dried rosemary over the chicken — or, if you're using fresh rosemary, pull the leaves off the stalk, put them in a cup, snip them into small pieces, then scatter them over the chicken.

4 Sprinkle some pepper over the chicken. Then, put the casserole on the high shelf in the oven for 30 minutes.

5 Meanwhile, peel the onion and chop it into small pieces. Cut the top off the bell pepper. Cut the bell pepper in half. Pull out the seeds and white parts. Cut the bell pepper into bite-sized chunks.

6 Peel the skin from the garlic. Put the half bouillon cube in a heatproof measuring cup and pour in ⅔ cup boiling water. Stir until the cube dissolves.

7 Use a vegetable peeler to peel a strip of zest from the lemon. Cut the lemon in half and squeeze the juice from one half. Save the other half for another recipe.

8 Put the remaining oil, the onion and bell pepper in a saucepan. Cook on medium heat for 5 minutes, stirring often. Crush in the garlic and cook for 1 minute.

9 Put the canned tomatoes, lemon zest, lemon juice and bouillon in the pan with the onion and bell pepper. Stir the sauce, then leave it to simmer for 10 minutes.

10 When the chicken has cooked for 30 minutes, take it out of the oven. Pour the sauce in, then put the casserole back in the oven for another 30 minutes.

Kebabs

Ingredients:

For the marinade:

1 lemon

4 tablespoons of olive oil

1 pinch of crushed red pepper (optional)

1 clove of garlic

2 sprigs of fresh parsley (optional)

For the kebabs:

2-3 skinless, boneless chicken breasts (12-14oz. in total)

1 red onion

1 red or yellow bell pepper

1 zucchini

You will also need 8 wooden or metal barbecue skewers

Serves 4

Kebabs are pieces of meat, vegetables or other things cooked on skewers. In this recipe, you leave the meat in a liquid called a marinade, to give it more flavor (see page 89).

1 If you're using wooden skewers, put them in a pan and cover them with water. This will help to stop them from burning when you cook your kebabs.

2 To make the marinade, cut the lemon in half, squeeze out the juice and put it in a large bowl. Add the olive oil and crushed red pepper. Peel the garlic and crush it in, too.

3 Pick the leaves off the parsley stalks. Put the leaves in a cup. Snip them into tiny pieces. Put them in the bowl with the other marinade ingredients.

4 Put half the marinade in a small bowl. Cut the chicken into pieces around ½ inch wide. Put them in the large bowl. Stir, cover the bowl with food wrap, and refrigerate for an hour, or longer.

5 Meanwhile, prepare the vegetables. Peel the onion and cut it in half, then into quarters. Cut across each quarter. Then, separate each chunk into single slices, like this.

6 Cut the top off the bell pepper. Cut the bell pepper in half and then into quarters. Remove the seeds and white parts. Cut the bell pepper into chunks around ½ inch wide.

7 Cut the ends off the zucchini and throw them away. Then cut the zucchini into slices around ¼ inch thick.

8 Push a piece of chicken onto a skewer. Add pieces of vegetable and more chicken. Fill the skewers, and use up all the chicken and vegetables.

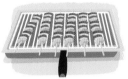

9 Turn the broiler to medium and leave it for 5 minutes to heat up. Put the kebabs in the broiler pan. Brush over some marinade from the small bowl.

10 Broil for 10 minutes. Then turn the kebabs over and brush with more marinade. Broil for 5-10 more minutes.

11 Test a piece of chicken. Cut through it. It should be white all the way through. If there is any pink, broil for 5-10 minutes more and test again.

Lamb or beef kebabs

Replace the chicken with 12-14 oz. lamb steak, or beef such as round steak.

Follow steps 1-3. At step 4, cut any fat or bone off the meat. Cut the meat into 1 inch cubes. Follow steps 5-10. Check the meat is cooked through.

Fish kebabs

You will need the marinade ingredients plus 12-14 oz. skinless fillets of fish such as salmon or haddock, 1 red or yellow bell pepper, 1 cup baby Bella mushrooms and 16 cherry tomatoes.

Follow steps 1-3. At step 4, cut the fish into 1 inch chunks and stir them into the marinade. Prepare the bell pepper as in step 6. Push the fish and vegetables onto the skewers. Follow steps 9 and 10. Then, check the fish to make sure it is the same color and firm in texture all the way through.

Cheese kebabs

You will need all the ingredients for the marinade plus 1 lb. halloumi (grilling cheese), 1 red or yellow bell pepper, 1 cup baby Bella mushrooms and around 16 cherry tomatoes.

Follow steps 1-3. At step 4 cut the halloumi into 1 inch chunks and put them in the marinade. Prepare the pepper as in step 6. Push the halloumi and vegetables onto the skewers. Cook following steps 9-10, but only cook for 7 minutes for the first side and 5 minutes for the second.

Roasted chicken

Ingredients:

1 lemon

3 or 4 sprigs of fresh thyme (optional)

1 bay leaf

1 roasting chicken, around 3½lbs.

1 tablespoon of olive oil

You will also need:

a roasting pan

a large piece of aluminum foil,
  around 30 inches long

Serves 4

A roasted chicken is easier to cook than you might think. You could roast some vegetables in the oven at the same time (page 38), but cook the vegetables for 10 minutes longer than the recipe there says.

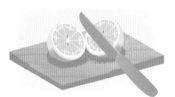

1 Preheat the oven to 375°F. Cut the lemon in half.

2 Lay the middle of the foil over the roasting pan. Gently press the foil down to line the pan, leaving the two foil ends sticking out at either side.

3 Remove any packaging from the chicken, including any ties on the legs. Then, put the chicken in the roasting pan with the breast side down.

4 Tuck the lemon, bay leaf and thyme inside the chicken. Then use your hands to rub the oil all over the chicken. Wash your hands well.

5 Put the roasting pan in the oven. After 45 minutes, lift it out carefully, wearing oven mitts. Still wearing the mitts, take hold of the ends of the foil.

6 Pull one end of the foil gently upwards, like this, to roll the chicken slowly over. Then, cut off the longer end of the foil.

7 Carefully tilt the pan so the juices run to one end. Spoon them all over the chicken. This will help to keep it moist.

Other sizes of chicken

If your chicken is bigger or smaller than 3½lbs. you'll need to change the cooking times. First, check the weight of your chicken. For every 1lb. it weighs, cook it for 20 minutes. Then, add 15 minutes at the end of the cooking time. So, for example, cook a 3lb. chicken for 1 hour and 15 minutes. After half the cooking time, turn your chicken over, as in step 6.

8 Roast the chicken for 45 minutes more. Check it every now and then. If it looks dry, spoon the juices over it again.

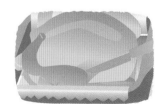

9 When the cooking time is up, push the point of a sharp knife into the meat beside the leg. If the meat looks at all pink, cook it for another 10 minutes.

10 The chicken is cooked when the meat is all white. Push a wooden spoon into the cavity and lift the chicken onto a warm plate. Leave it for 10 minutes before cutting it into pieces.

Beef stew

Ingredients:

For the stew:

1lb. lean chuck steak,
   cut into cubes

2½ tablespoons of cornstarch

¼ teaspoon of ground allspice

1 large onion or 12 small shallots

3 large carrots or 9 baby carrots

2 cloves of garlic

1 bay leaf

½ beef bouillon cube

2½ tablespoons of tomato paste

2½ tablespoons of balsamic vinegar

2 teaspoons of Dijon mustard (optional)

2 cups green beans or broccoli,
   cut into bite-sized chunks

For the dumplings:

1½ cups self-rising flour

½ stick (¼ cup) chilled butter

2 teaspoons of Dijon mustard (optional)

You will also need a large ovenproof
   casserole dish with a lid.

Serves 4

To make shallots easier to peel,
put them in a heatproof bowl
and cover with boiling water.
Leave for 10 minutes, drain
and cool, before you peel them.

This rich and warming stew is perfect for a cold day. The recipe includes dumplings — little doughy balls that cook on top of the stew. If you prefer, you could add potatoes instead — just follow the instructions on the opposite page.

1 Preheat your oven to 325°F.

2 Cut any white fat off the meat and cut up any big pieces. Put the cornstarch and allspice in the casserole. Put the meat in too and mix it around.

3 If you're using an onion, peel it and chop it into small pieces. If you're using shallots, peel them and pull off any hairy roots. Put the onion or shallots in the casserole.

4 Scrub or peel the carrots. Cut large carrots into bite-sized pieces but leave baby ones whole. Put the carrots in the cassserole. Peel the garlic and crush it in, too. Add the bay leaf and some pepper.

5 Put the half bouillon cube in a heatproof measuring cup. Add the tomato paste, vinegar and mustard. Pour in 2½ cups boiling water. Stir until the cube dissolves. Pour the mixture into the casserole and stir.

Leave a small gap.

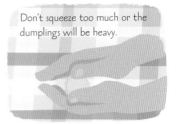

Don't squeeze too much or the dumplings will be heavy.

6 Put the casserole on medium heat and put on a lid. When the stew starts to boil, turn off the heat and put the casserole in the oven, with the lid on. Cook for 2 hours.

7 Meanwhile, make the dumplings. Put the flour in a bowl. Cut up the butter and add it too. Rub the butter into the flour with your fingertips and thumbs, until the mixture looks like fine breadcrumbs (see page 149).

8 Mix the mustard with 3½ tablespoons of cold water. Sprinkle this into the bowl. Stir until the mixture starts to stick together. Shape it into 12 small balls.

10 Put the casserole back in the oven without the lid. Cook for 20-25 minutes more, or until the dumplings are golden-brown and the meat is tender.

The bay leaf is for flavoring only. It's best to avoid eating it, as it's hard and tastes bitter.

9 When the stew has cooked for 2 hours, stir in the beans or broccoli. Put the dumplings on top of the stew. They shouldn't touch each other.

Stew with potatoes

Extra ingredients: 1lb. small new potatoes or medium-sized potatoes.

Scrub or peel the potatoes. Cut any medium-sized ones into quarters. Follow steps 1-4. Put the potatoes in the dish. Follow steps 5-6. Skip to step 9 (leaving out the dumplings). Put the casserole back in the oven without the lid for 20-25 minutes more.

Sticky ribs

Ingredients:

12 meaty pork ribs, around
   2lbs. total

2½ tablespoons of red wine vinegar

For the barbecue glaze:

2½ tablespoons of red wine vinegar

2½ tablespoons of light brown sugar

2½ tablespoons of orange juice

2½ tablespoons of soy sauce (or wheat-
   and gluten-free tamari sauce)

1 tablespoon of vegetable oil

1 tablespoon of tomato paste

1 tablespoon of Dijon mustard

1 large pinch of crushed red pepper
   or 1 teaspoon of mild chili powder

1 clove of garlic

You will also need some aluminum foil

Serves 4

This recipe shows how to cook pork ribs in a sticky, barbecue-flavor glaze. You could eat them with cooked corn on the cob (see opposite) and crunchy homemade coleslaw (page 29).

1 Put the ribs in a large saucepan. Pour in just enough cold water to cover them. Then, add the vinegar. Put the pan on medium heat.

2 When the water boils, turn down the heat so the water bubbles gently. Cook for 20 minutes. Now and then, use a spoon to scoop off any foam that forms.

3 While the ribs are cooking, make the glaze. Mix the vinegar, sugar, orange juice, soy sauce, oil, tomato paste, mustard and red pepper in a small saucepan. Crush in the garlic.

4 Put the pan on medium heat. When it boils, turn down the heat so it bubbles gently. Cook for 2-3 minutes, until the mixture has thickened slightly.

5 Preheat the oven to 400°F. Carefully drain the ribs in a large colander. Then use tongs to arrange them in a single layer in a large roasting pan.

6 Brush sauce all over each rib. Then, cover the roasting pan with aluminum foil and bake for 20 minutes.

7 Take the ribs out of the oven and remove the foil. Brush the ribs again with the rest of the sauce. Put them back in the oven without the foil and cook for another 15 minutes, or until the ribs are dark brown and sticky.

Five-spice ribs

For Chinese-style ribs, use sesame oil instead of vegetable oil (except if you have a nut allergy), 1 teaspoon of ground ginger instead of mustard and 2 teaspoons of Chinese five-spice powder instead of crushed red pepper.

Corn on the cob

You will need 1 whole or 2 half ears of corn per person. If the corn is still in its leaves, remove them and any silky threads. Fill a large pan with water and put it on medium heat. When the water boils, carefully lower in the corn cobs. Turn down the heat, so the water boils gently. Put a lid on (leave a gap). Cook for 8-10 minutes, until the corn is tender. Drain it and leave it to cool slightly. Wrap the ends of a cob in a paper napkin and bite off the kernels.

About fish

Some people think cooking fish is difficult, but it can be incredibly quick and easy, and it's good for you, too. These pages will give you some advice on how to prepare and cook different types of fish.

Seafood

Food from rivers or the sea is known as seafood. This includes fish, such as tuna and salmon, and shellfish, such as mussels and shrimp. Some seafood is sold fresh, but other types, such as canned fish or pink shrimp, are already cooked. You can also buy frozen seafood.

Herbs for seafood

Parsley, dill weed and bay leaves go well with seafood. Lemon, lime and other citrus fruits and pepper can work well, too.

Defrosting shrimp

To defrost frozen shrimp, put them in a strainer and rinse them under cold water. When they're defrosted, pat them dry with paper towels.

Whole or not

Fish can be sold whole, partly cut up or completely prepared. Pieces of fish with the bones removed are called fillets. But it's still best to check for any tiny bones (see below).

Fish safety

Some types of fresh seafood can be eaten raw. But, for the recipes here, it's best to cook seafood thoroughly. Wash your hands and any knives and cutting boards, too.

Removing bones

Before you cook fish fillets, run your fingers gently all over them. Pull out any bones you can feel, and throw them away.

Poaching fish

1 To cook a fish fillet in water or milk, put the fish in a large saucepan. Make sure the pieces are in one layer and don't overlap. Pour in enough water or milk to cover them.

2 Put the pan on medium heat. When the water boils, turn down the heat so it bubbles gently. Cook for around 8 minutes.

3 Take the pan off the heat. Using a spatula, lift the fish onto a plate. Check to see if it is cooked all the way through (see below).

Pan-frying fish

1 To pan-fry fish fillets, put a non-stick frying pan on high heat for 1 minute. Pour in a little olive oil (around ½ tablespoon for each piece of fish).

2 Tip the pan so the oil covers the bottom. Add the fish fillets and cook them for around 3 minutes.

3 Use a spatula to turn the fillets over. Cook for the same time on the other side. Check they are cooked through — they should still be moist, not dry.

Is it cooked?

To find out if a piece of fish is cooked, cut into the middle. It should be firm and flaky and the same color all the way through. If there are any slightly see-through parts, cook for just a little longer, then test again.

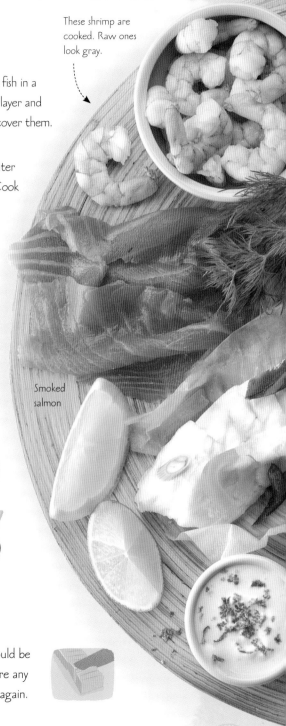

These shrimp are cooked. Raw ones look gray.

Smoked salmon

Fishcakes

Ingredients:

12oz. fresh fillets of white fish such as cod, tilapia or flounder

3 or 4 sprigs of fresh parsley or cilantro (optional)

1 bay leaf

1lb. potatoes

1 tablespoon butter, margarine or dairy-free spread

7 tablespoons of all-purpose flour or cornmeal (corn flour)

Serves 4

Fishcakes are basically flakes of fish, mixed with mashed potatoes and patted into small, round cake shapes. This recipe shows how to cook fresh fish for your fishcakes, but you can use canned fish instead — just follow the instructions on the opposite page.

1 Put the fish in a large saucepan in one layer — don't overlap the pieces. Pour in just enough water to cover them.

2 Break the stalks off the parsley or cilantro and put them in the pan. Put the bay leaf in too. Heat until the water boils, then turn down the heat so it bubbles gently.

3 Cook the fish for 4 minutes, then take the pan off the heat. Using a spatula, lift the fish out and put it on a plate to cool. Leave the water in the pan.

4 Scrub or peel the potatoes and cut them into large chunks. Put them in the pan and heat until the water boils. Turn down the heat so the water bubbles gently. Cook for 15-20 minutes, or until the potatoes are tender.

5 While the potatoes are cooking, peel any skin off the fish and throw it away. Break the fish into flakes with a fork. As you do so, look out for any bones and remove them.

6 Drain the potatoes in a colander, then pour them back into the pan. Add the butter, a pinch of salt and some pepper. Mash until the mixture is smooth and fluffy.

7 Put the parsley or cilantro leaves in a cup and snip them up with scissors. Put them in the pan with the potatoes and add the fish. Stir until everything is well mixed.

Different fish

You could replace the white fish in this recipe with the same weight of fresh salmon fillets, or smoked fish such as smoked haddock fillets.

Quick fishcakes

Replace the fresh fish with a can of fish such as salmon, weighing around 7oz.

Skip steps 1-3. Scrub or peel the potatoes, chop them up, put them in a pan and cover them with water. Cook until tender. While they are cooking, drain the canned fish and put it on a plate. Flake it with a fork, removing any skin and bones. Then, follow steps 6-10.

You could put some flour on your hands to stop the mixture from sticking.

8 Divide the mixture into 8-10 pieces. Pat each piece into a round shape that's slightly flattened and around ¾ inch thick.

9 Put the flour or cornmeal in a bowl. Roll each fishcake around, until it's covered. Put 1 tablespoon of cooking oil in a frying pan.

10 Put the pan on medium heat. After 3 minutes, add the fishcakes. Cook for 5 minutes, then turn the fishcakes over and cook for 5 minutes more, until they are golden-brown all over.

Fish in a packet

Ingredients:

1 lemon

½ bouillon stock cube

1⅓ cups couscous

2 green onions

12 cherry tomatoes

1 red or yellow bell pepper or 1 zucchini

1 teaspoon of olive oil

4 firm fish fillets (such as salmon or flounder) each around 5oz.

You will also need 4 large squares of aluminum foil or parchment paper, each around 12 inches square.

Serves 4

If you wrap fish up in aluminum foil or parchment paper before cooking it in the oven, it stays deliciously moist. Add some couscous and vegetables and you have a meal in a packet.

1 Preheat the oven to 400°F. Grate the zest from the lemon using the small holes on a grater. Then, squeeze the juice from one half.

2 Put the half bouillon cube in a heatproof measuring cup. Pour in 1 cup boiling water. Stir until the cube has dissolved completely.

3 Put the couscous and lemon zest in a heatproof bowl. Pour in the hot bouillon. Cover the bowl with a plate or saucepan lid and leave it for 5 minutes.

4 Meanwhile, cut the roots and most of the dark green parts off the green onions. Cut the rest into small pieces. Cut each cherry tomato in half.

5 If you're using a bell pepper, cut off the top and cut the bell pepper in half. Pull out any seeds and white pith. Cut the halves into quarters and cut the quarters into thin strips.

6 If you're using a zucchini, cut off the ends and throw them away. Then, cut the zucchini into lots of thin strips.

7 The couscous should have absorbed all the bouillon by now. Take off the lid or plate and stir with a fork to separate the grains. Add the vegetables and mix them in.

8 Run your fingers over each fish fillet. If you feel any little bones sticking out, pull them out and throw them away.

9 Brush the olive oil over the foil or parchment squares. Divide the vegetables and couscous between the squares. Put a fish fillet on top of each pile. Add the lemon juice.

10 Bring together the top and bottom edges of each square. Fold over their edges twice. Then, fold up both sides of each square twice, to seal the packet.

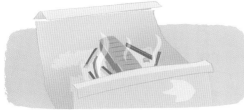 

11 Put the packets on a cookie sheet and bake for 15-20 minutes. Lift out the cookie sheet and let them cool for 5 minutes. Then, open a packet very carefully, watching out for hot steam escaping.

12 Cut open the fish to make sure it's cooked. It should be the same color all the way through. If there are any parts that are slightly see-through, put all the packets back in the oven for another 5-10 minutes, then check again.

Other flavors

You could use soy or wheat- and gluten-free tamari sauce instead of lemon. Follow steps 1-6, leaving out the lemon. Put the vegetables in a bowl, add 1 tablespoon of olive oil, 1 teaspoon of balsamic vinegar, 2 teaspoons of soy or tamari sauce and 1 crushed clove of garlic. Mix, then add to the couscous in step 7. Follow steps 8-12.

Coconut shrimp

Ingredients:

1½ cups large cooked shrimp, fresh or frozen

4 shallots

2 cloves of garlic

1 tablespoon of vegetable oil

½ teaspoon of ground coriander seed

½ teaspoon of ground cumin

¼-½ teaspoon of crushed red pepper (depending on how hot you like your food)

a piece of fresh ginger around 1inch long

a medium sized bunch of fresh cilantro (around 1oz.)

2 tablespoons of Thai fish sauce

2 stalks of fresh lemongrass

1⅔ cups coconut milk (not beverage coconut milk) (coconut milk may not be suitable for those with nut allergies)

1½ cups sugarsnap peas (snow peas)

a few basil leaves (optional)

1 lime (optional)

Serves 4

With rice

To serve your coconut shrimp with boiled or steamed rice, follow the instructions on page 115. Start cooking it before or after step 3, depending on the cooking times on the packaging.

Shrimp are quick to cook, and have a delicate taste that goes well with creamy and spicy ingredients. This mild, Thai-style shrimp curry is made with coconut milk. It's delicious served with boiled or steamed rice (see below).

1 If you're using frozen shrimp, defrost them (see page 104). If you're using fresh shrimp, put them in a strainer and leave it over the sink to drain.

2 Cut the ends off the shallots, then peel off the papery skin. Cut each shallot in half, then cut the halves into thin slices and the slices into small pieces. Peel the papery skin from the garlic.

3 Put the oil in a large saucepan. Put the pan on medium heat. Put in the shallots, crush in the garlic and add the coriander, cumin and red pepper. Cook for 10 minutes or until the shallots are soft.

4 Cut the brown skin off the ginger and throw it away. Grate the ginger on the fine holes of a grater, then scrape it into the pan.

5 Pick the leaves off the cilantro stalks. Put the leaves in a cup and snip them into small pieces. Put the chopped cilantro in the pan. Add the fish sauce, too.

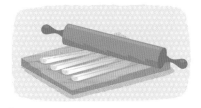

6 Remove the outer layer from each stalk of lemongrass. Cut each stalk in half lengthways. Use a rolling pin to roll over the stalks, to release the flavor.

7 Put the lemongrass and coconut milk in the pan. When the mixture starts to boil, turn down the heat a little so it bubbles gently. Leave it to bubble for 5 minutes. Then, use a wooden spoon to lift out the pieces of lemongrass. Throw them away.

8 Add the sugarsnap peas. Cook for 3 minutes. Stir in the shrimp and cook for 2 more minutes. Add the basil leaves. Cut the lime into wedges, to squeeze over the coconut shrimp as you eat.

Fish sticks

Ingredients:

½ cup cornmeal (corn flour)

1 large egg

1lb. skinless, firm fish fillets (such as salmon, flounder or cod)

Serves 4

Lime mayonnaise

You will need 1 lime, 4 tablespoons of mayonnaise and a sprig of fresh parsley, dill weed or cilantro (optional). Squeeze the juice from the lime and put it in a bowl with the mayonnaise and a pinch of pepper. Snip up the herb leaves and mix them in.

Breadcrumb coating

You could replace the cornmeal with 3 slices of bread made into breadcrumbs (page 135).

These fish sticks have a crispy coating made of cornmeal. They taste good with lime mayonnaise.

1 Preheat the oven to 400°F. Use a paper towel to wipe a little oil over a roasting pan.

2 Put the cornmeal in a wide dish. Add a pinch of salt and some pepper and mix them in.

3 Break the egg into another dish. Beat it with a fork to mix the white and yolk together.

4 Cut the fish into strips around ¾ inch wide and 4 inches long. Dip a strip in the egg, to coat it.

5 Roll the strip in the cornmeal, until it's covered. Put it in the roasting pan. Do this with all the strips.

6 Bake for 5 minutes, then turn the fish sticks over. Bake for 5 more minutes, until crisp and golden.

Rice & beans

Find out how to cook rice by boiling or steaming it.

Cook lamb tagine, a chickpea stew flavored with cinnamon and apricots.

About rice

Rice is the grain, or seed, of a plant that's a little similar to wheat. Rice has been grown as food for thousands of years in some parts of the world. Here you can find some useful advice about cooking with rice.

Different types

There are many different varieties of rice. Some have long grains, some have short grains, some stay separate and some become sticky during cooking. Rice is almost always sold dried. It keeps like this for a long time, so it's a good food to store in your kitchen pantry.

Converted or not

Rice labeled 'converted' has been partly cooked already. There are different types of converted rice, from basmati to Italian rice. If you're using rice that's not converted, you may need to rinse or soak it first. Check what the packaging says.

Polished rice

Most rice has been 'polished' to remove the outer layers. Brown rice has had fewer layers removed, so it contains more natural goodness, but it may take longer to cook.

Brown rice like this has a pleasant, slightly nutty taste.

This rice has been 'converted' to make it quicker to cook .

This is risotto rice. It becomes sticky when it's cooked.

Boiling rice

1 Allow around ½ cup rice per person. Half fill a pan with water. Put the pan on medium heat. When the water boils, add the rice.

2 Wait until the water boils again, then turn down the heat so it is bubbling gently. Cook for as long as it says on the packaging. Drain the rice in a strainer.

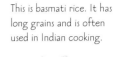

This is basmati rice. It has long grains and is often used in Indian cooking.

Wild rice like this needs to be soaked and then cooked for a long time.

Sticky rice?

If your boiled rice sticks together in a soggy clump, put it in a strainer and pour over 4 cups of boiling water. This will help to wash away the stickiness.

Cooked rice

Once rice has been cooked, it can go bad very quickly. It's best to eat cooked rice right away — avoid storing it to use later.

Steaming rice

1 Measure ½ cup of rice and 1 cup of water per person into a saucepan. Cook on medium heat. When the water boils, stir the rice.

2 Turn down the heat a little, so the water bubbles gently. Then, put on a lid and cook for as long as it says on the packaging.

3 Try not to lift the lid to check on the rice, as this lets some of the water escape as steam. If any water is left at the end, cook for another minute or two.

Fried rice

Ingredients:

½ vegetable bouillon cube

1 cup converted long-grain rice

6 green onions

2 large eggs (optional)

2 tablespoons of cooking oil such
  as vegetable oil

1 cup frozen peas

¾ cup chopped ham
  (optional)

2 teaspoons of soy sauce (or wheat-
  and gluten-free tamari sauce)

Serves 4

This Chinese-style fried rice is really a meal in itself, but you could eat it with a main dish such as the five-spice sticky ribs on page 103. In this recipe, the rice is flavored with peas, ham and eggs, but you could trade them for other ingredients — see the suggestions on the opposite page.

1 Half fill a large saucepan with water and put it on high heat. Crumble in the half bouillon cube.

2 When the water boils, pour in the rice. Wait until the water starts to boil again, then turn down the heat until it is bubbling gently. Leave the rice to cook for as long as it says on the packaging.

4 Break the eggs into a cup, add 1 teaspoon of the oil and whisk everything together with a fork.

3 While the rice is cooking, trim the roots and most of the dark green parts off the green onions. Snip the green onions into small pieces.

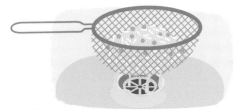

5 When the rice is cooked, turn off the heat. Add the peas and stir. Then, drain the rice and peas in a large strainer.

6 Put the rest of the oil in a wok or a large frying pan. Cook on medium heat for 1 minute. Then, add the green onions. Stir them around in the hot oil for 3 minutes or until they are soft.

7 Add the cooked rice and peas, ham and soy sauce and stir them around for 2-3 minutes, to heat them up.

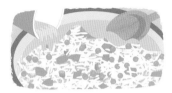

8 Push the rice mixture to one side of the pan. Pour the egg mixture into the other side and leave for around 20 seconds, so it begins to set.

9 Using a wooden spoon, stir the egg mixture quickly to break it up, then stir it into the rice mixture. Keep stirring and cooking for another minute. Eat right away.

Variations

You could add any of these to your fried rice:

- 2 handfuls of sliced white mushrooms, added in step 6 with the green onions

- a handful of chopped, cooked chicken (such as leftover roast chicken), added in step 7

- a handful of cooked shrimp, added at step 7

- a handful of toasted cashew nuts, added at step 7

- 2 cloves of garlic, crushed and added in step 6 after the green onions have been cooking for 2 minutes

- a handful of bean sprouts, added at step 7

Stuffed bell peppers

Ingredients:

For the stuffed bell peppers:

½ vegetable bouillon cube

4 red or yellow bell peppers,
   or a mixture

1 onion

1 tablespoon of olive oil

1 clove of garlic

½ teaspoon ground cumin

⅔ cup converted long-grain or
   converted basmati rice

a few sprigs of fresh oregano or parsley

5oz. Cheddar or other hard
   cheese (optional)

½ a 15oz. can of red kidney beans

For the spicy tomato sauce:

2 cloves of garlic

1 tablespoon of olive oil

a 14oz. can of diced tomatoes

2½ tablespoons of tomato paste

1 pinch of sugar

1 large pinch of crushed red pepper or
   1 teaspoon of chili powder (optional)

You will also need:

a small ovenproof pan or roasting pan
a large piece of aluminum foil

Serves 4

This recipe shows how to cook bell peppers stuffed with a mixture of rice, beans and cheese, and make a spicy tomato sauce to eat with them.

For a dairy-free version, leave out the cheese, or replace it with the same amount of chopped salami or drained, canned tuna.

1 Preheat the oven to 350°F. Pour 1⅔ cups boiling water into a heatproof measuring cup and crumble in the half bouillon cube. Stir until the cube has dissolved.

2 Cut the tops off the bell peppers and pull out the seeds and white parts. Then, peel the onion, cut it in half, then into quarters. Cut the quarters into slices and the slices into small pieces.

3 Heat the oil in a saucepan for 1 minute. Add the onion and cook on medium heat for 5 minutes. Crush the garlic into the pan, add the cumin and rice and stir for a few seconds.

4 Pour 1½ cups of the bouillon over the rice mixture. When it boils, turn down the heat to low. Cover the pan with a lid and cook for 12 minutes, or until the bouillon has been absorbed by the rice.

5 While the rice is cooking, pick the leaves off the oregano or parsley stalks. Put the leaves in a cup and snip them into tiny pieces using kitchen scissors. Cut the cheese into ½ inch cubes.

6 Put the kidney beans in a strainer. Rinse and drain them well. Stir the beans, chopped oregano or parsley and cheese into the rice.

7 Stand the bell peppers upright in your ovenproof pan. Spoon the rice mixture into the peppers and press it down lightly with the spoon. Put the tops back on the bell peppers.

8 Pour the rest of the stock into the pan around the peppers. Tightly cover the pan with foil and bake for 55 minutes, or until the bell peppers are soft.

9 While the bell peppers are cooking, make the chili tomato sauce, following the instructions on page 32. Eat the sauce with the bell peppers.

Paella

Ingredients:

4oz. spicy sausage such as chorizo

2 skinless, boneless chicken breasts,
   or 4 skinless, boneless chicken thighs

1 onion

4 ripe tomatoes

1 cup frozen peas

1½ chicken or vegetable bouillon cubes

1 tablespoon of olive oil

1 clove of garlic

1 cup paella rice such as Arborio
   or Valencia

1 pinch of saffron strands or
   ½ teaspoon of ground turmeric

1 cup large cooked, shelled shrimp
   or a mix of seafood such as shrimp
   calamari and mussels

Serves 4

In Spain, paella is often
cooked in a wide, flat pan,
also known as a paella.
But you can use a large
saucepan, frying pan or wok.

Paella is a Spanish dish. It's made with rice and can be flavored with different types of meat and fish. This recipe is for paella with chicken, shrimp and a Spanish sausage called chorizo. For a vegetarian version, you could leave these out and stir in a drained can of chickpeas at step 9.

You could serve your paella with a
wedge of lemon to squeeze over
it as you eat.

1 Chop the chorizo sausage and the chicken into bite-sized chunks.

2 Peel the onion and cut off the root. Cut it in half, then cut the halves into slices. Cut the slices into small pieces.

3 Cut each tomato in half, then cut the halves into quarters. Cut out the green cores. Then cut the quarters into small pieces.

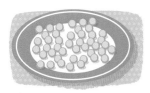

4 Spread the frozen peas in a single layer on a plate and leave them to defrost.

5 Put the bouillon cubes in a heatproof measuring cup. Add 4 cups boiling water and stir until they dissolve.

6 Heat the oil in a large pan on medium heat for around 30 seconds. Add the chorizo and cook, stirring, for 2 minutes. Add the chicken and cook for 2 more minutes, or until the chicken is white all over.

7 Using a slotted spoon, lift the chicken and chorizo out of the pan and onto a plate, leaving all the fat behind in the pan. Add the onion and crush the garlic into the pan. Cook for 5 minutes, stirring often.

8 Stir in the rice and saffron strands or turmeric. Stir for 30 seconds, then pour in the bouillon. Bring to a boil, then stir and turn down the heat. Cover with a lid and cook for 15 minutes.

9 Stir in the chicken and chorizo, put the lid back on the pan and cook for 10 minutes. Then, stir in the shrimp, peas and chopped tomatoes. Cover with the lid and cook for another 5 minutes.

10 Take off the lid. The rice should have absorbed the bouillon and be tender. If not, let the mixture bubble for a further 2-3 minutes, or until the rice is cooked.

Risotto

Ingredients:

1½ cups baby Bella mushrooms

1 onion

2 stalks of celery (optional)

1 large clove of garlic

2oz. Parmesan cheese (or ¾ cup grated Parmesan)

1 vegetable bouillon cube

1 tablespoon of butter

1 tablespoon of olive oil

1 cup risotto rice such as Arborio

1 pinch of ground nutmeg (optional)

Serves 4

Shrimp & pea risotto

Replace the mushrooms, Parmesan and nutmeg with 1 cup cooked, shelled shrimp, ½ cup frozen peas and 1 tablespoon extra butter. Spread the peas on a plate to defrost. Follow steps 2-5 (leaving out the cheese). Then, take the pan off the heat, add the rice and stir. Follow steps 7-8. Add the shrimp and peas and cook for 3 minutes. Then, follow step 9, leaving out the cheese and nutmeg but adding the extra butter.

Risotto is an Italian dish made from a sticky type of rice cooked with vegetables and bouillon. As the rice cooks, some of its stickiness leaks out into the bouillon, making a delicious, thick sauce. This recipe shows how to make a mushroom risotto. There are instructions below for adapting the recipe to make a shrimp and pea risotto.

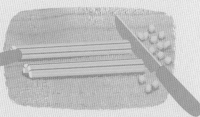

1 Wipe the mushrooms with a damp paper towel. Cut them into slices around the same thickness as a pencil.

2 Peel the onion and cut off the ends. Cut it in half, then cut the halves into fine slices, and cut the slices into small pieces.

3 Wash the celery stalks and cut them lengthways into thin strips. Cut across the strips to make small pieces. Then, peel the garlic clove.

4 Grate the cheese on the fine holes of a grater. Put the bouillon cube in a heatproof measuring cup and pour on 4 cups of boiling water. Stir until the cube dissolves.

5 Put the butter, oil, onion and celery in a large saucepan or frying pan. Crush in the garlic. Cook on medium heat for 5 minutes, or until the onion is soft.

6 Put the mushrooms in the pan and cook for another 5 minutes, until they have softened. Take the pan off the heat. Pour in the rice and stir to coat it in the pan juices.

7 Put the pan back on the heat, then pour in all the bouillon. Give the mixture a good stir, wait until it starts to bubble, then turn the heat down so it bubbles gently.

8 Cook for 30 minutes, stirring often. Stir more and more towards the end of the cooking time, so it doesn't stick to the bottom of the pan. When the rice is tender, it is cooked.

9 Take the pan off the heat, put on a lid and leave for 3 minutes. Grate in some nutmeg, grind in some pepper and add the Parmesan. Stir well.

About beans

Here you can find out about dried and canned beans, lentils and corn. You'll also find some useful hints on how to prepare them, and how to cook them.

Beans & other things

Dried beans usually need to be soaked in water and then boiled for a long time. The instructions on the packaging will tell you how. Beans sold in cans have already been soaked and cooked, so you can use them right away.

Lentils

Lentils are related to beans. You can buy some lentils in cans, but most are sold dried. Some need to be soaked before they are cooked, and some need to be rinsed. Check the instructions on the package if you're not sure.

Corn

Corn isn't a type of bean, but it can be used in similar ways. It can be eaten fresh, or dried and ground into cornmeal or cornstarch. Cornmeal is used in the recipes on pages 112 and 178. You'll find instructions for cooking corn on the cob on page 103.

Sugar and salt

Some canned beans, lentils and corn have salt and sugar added to the liquid in the can. It's best to choose types canned in plain water.

Adding salt

If you're cooking dried beans or lentils, wait until they are cooked before adding salt. Salt added during cooking may toughen them.

Individual pieces of corn are known as kernels.

This is cornmeal, or corn flour.

These are canned chickpeas.

These are dried navy beans. They're the beans you find in cans of baked beans.

These are dried cranberry beans.

Heating canned beans or corn

1 To heat canned beans or corn, put the contents of the can, including the liquid, in a pan. Put it on medium heat.

2 When the liquid bubbles, turn the heat down to low and cook for 5 minutes. You may want to drain off the liquid.

These are red lentils. They're used in the spicy lentil recipe on page 126.

Cooking dried beans or lentils

1 Check the instructions on the packaging to find out if you need to rinse or soak the beans or lentils. Put them in a saucepan, cover with cold water and put the pan on medium heat.

2 When the water boils, turn the heat to low, so the water bubbles gently. Cook for as long as it says on the packaging, or until they are tender.

Mashing beans

Mashed canned beans, such as butter beans or cranberry beans, make a tasty side dish. Heat the beans following the instructions above, then take the pan off the heat and use a potato masher to mash them into a rough paste. Then, stir in some chopped fresh parsley, a pinch of salt and some pepper. See also page 51 for a recipe for refried beans.

Spicy lentils

Ingredients:

1½ cups frozen peas or
  edamame beans

a 1 inch piece of fresh ginger

1 small eggplant

1 large carrot

1 medium potato

1⅓ cups red lentils

1 vegetable bouillon cube

1 onion

2½ tablespoons of vegetable oil

1 teaspoon of brown mustard
  seeds (optional)

2 teaspoons of ground coriander seed

2 teaspoons of ground cumin

½ teaspoon of ground turmeric

1 pinch of crushed red pepper

1 lemon

Serves 4

If you can't find brown
mustard seeds, use yellow
ones instead – they are
usually easier to find.

Lentils and spices go really well together. This recipe is inspired by an Indian dish called a sambar, made from beans or lentils and vegetables, and flavored with mustard seeds and other spices. Eat it with boiled or steamed rice (see page 115).

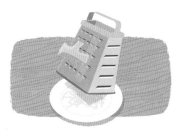

1 Spread the peas or edamame beans on a plate, to defrost. Then, cut the brown skin off the ginger and throw it away. Grate the ginger on the fine holes of a grater.

2 Cut the stalk off the eggplant and throw it away. Cut the eggplant in half lengthways. Cut the halves into strips and the strips into bite-sized chunks.

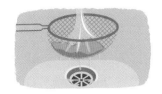

3 Scrub the carrot and the potato, or peel them if they are very muddy. Then cut them into small chunks around ¾ inch across.

4 Put the lentils in a strainer and rinse them under cold water. Leave them to drain over the sink.

5 Put the bouillon cube in a heatproof measuring cup. Add 3 cups boiling water and stir until the cube dissolves.

6 Peel the onion and chop it finely. Put it in a large saucepan with the oil. Cook on medium heat for 6-7 minutes.

7 Sprinkle over the mustard seeds, coriander, cumin, turmeric and red pepper and stir them in. Add the ginger and eggplant and cook for 2-3 minutes, until the onion is soft.

8 Add the carrot, potato and lentils, then pour in the bouillon. When the mixture boils, put a lid on the pan, leaving a small gap. Turn down the heat to low and cook for 20 minutes.

9 Squeeze the juice from the lemon. Add it to the mixture. Add the peas or edamame beans too, and stir everything together. Cook for 5 more minutes.

Other vegetables

You could replace the carrot, eggplant or potato with the same amounts of chopped sweet potato or cauliflower – add them at step 8. Or use trimmed green beans, small pieces of broccoli or snow peas instead of the edamame beans – add them at step 9 (cook for 5 minutes longer if you're using broccoli or beans).

With yogurt

In India, dishes like this one are often served with a yogurt side dish. You could just spoon some plain yogurt onto the side of your plate. Or, for a tastier version, strip the leaves from a few sprigs of cilantro and put the leaves in a cup. Use kitchen scissors to snip them into pieces, then stir the pieces into a small bowl of plain yogurt (around ⅔ cup).

Lamb tagine

Ingredients:

2 teaspoons of cornstarch

3 teaspoons of ground cinnamon

2 teaspoons of ground ginger

2 teaspoons of ground coriander seed

1/2 teaspoon of ground turmeric

1lb lean boneless lamb shoulder,
    boneless leg of lamb or lamb steaks

1 onion

2 cloves of garlic

1 lamb or vegetable bouillon cube

2 tablespoons of olive oil

a 15oz. can of diced tomatoes

1/2 cup soft dried apricots

a 15oz. can of chickpeas

For the couscous:

1 1/2 cups couscous

1 teaspoon of olive oil

(For a wheat- and gluten-free meal,
    serve with rice, not couscous.)

Serves 4

A tagine is a mild, spiced stew traditionally made in North Africa in a special pan, also called a tagine — though this recipe uses an ordinary saucepan. It's made with chickpeas and served with couscous, a fluffy, wheat-based grain.

1 Put the cornstarch, cinnamon, ginger, coriander and turmeric in a large bowl. Stir them together.

2 Cut any white fat off the lamb, then cut the meat into cubes. Put them in the bowl and stir to coat them in the spice mixture.

3 Leave the meat at room temperature for a few minutes or, if you have time, cover the bowl with plastic wrap and chill in the refrigerator for a few hours.

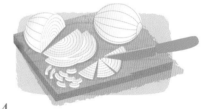

4 Peel the onion and cut off the ends. Cut the onion in half, then cut the halves into thin slices and the slices into small pieces. Peel the papery skin off the garlic.

5 Put the bouillon cube in a heatproof measuring cup. Pour on 1/2 cup boiling water. Stir until the cube has dissolved.

6 Heat 1 tablespoon of the oil in a large saucepan on medium-high heat for 3 minutes. Add the meat and cook for 3-4 minutes, turning, until it's browned on all sides. Turn down the heat, lift out the meat and put it on a plate.

7 Put the remaining tablespoon of oil in the pan. Add the onion and crush in the garlic. Cook for 5 minutes, stirring often. Stir in the diced tomatoes.

8 Put the meat back in the pan and add the bouillon and some pepper. Stir, then put on a lid. When the mixture boils, turn the heat to its lowest setting. Cook for 40 minutes.

You could add some fresh cilantro leaves to your tagine.

9 Snip the apricots in half. When the 40 minutes are up, take off the lid and stir in the apricots. Put the lid back on and cook for another 20 minutes, or until the meat is tender.

10 5 minutes before the tagine is ready, put the couscous in a heatproof bowl. Pour in 2 cups boiling water. Add the oil, stir, then cover with a pan lid.

11 Drain and rinse the chickpeas and stir them into the tagine. When the 5 minutes are up, use a fork to stir the couscous, to separate the grains. Serve it with the tagine.

Beef or chicken tagine

Replace the lamb with 1lb chuck steak or skinless, boneless chicken breast or skinless, boneless chicken thighs. You will need to cook the beef tagine for an extra 30-45 minutes at step 8.

Sweet potato tagine

Replace the lamb and cornstarch with 1lb sweet potatoes, peeled and cut into bite-sized chunks. Snip the dried apricots in half. Follow steps 4 and 5. Heat 1 tablespoon of oil in a large saucepan on medium heat. Add the onion, crush in the garlic, then add the cinnamon, ginger, coriander and turmeric. Cook for 5 minutes, stirring often. Stir in the tomatoes, bouillon, sweet potato, apricots and some pepper. Put on a lid. When the mixture boils, turn down the heat to the lowest setting. Cook for 20-25 minutes, or until the sweet potatoes are tender. Then follow steps 10 and 11.

Baked beans

Ingredients:

2 x 15oz. cans of navy beans

½ vegetable or beef bouillon cube

4 strips of thick bacon

1 onion

1 teaspoon of vegetable oil

1 clove of garlic

1 cup (canned) crushed tomatoes

2½ tablespoons of balsamic vinegar

1 tablespoon of dark brown sugar

1 teaspoon of Dijon mustard (optional)

Serves 4

Baked beans originally came from Boston, where they were cooked for hours with pork and molasses, a sweet, dark syrup made from sugar. This recipe uses canned beans, bacon and sugar instead. It's much quicker to cook, but the result is still really good.

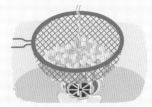

1 Open the cans of beans and put them in a strainer. Rinse them under cold water.

2 Put the half bouillon cube in a heatproof measuring cup. Add ½ cup boiling water. Stir until the cube dissolves.

3 Cut any fat off the edge of the bacon with scissors. Then, snip the bacon into small pieces.

4 Peel the onion and cut off the root. Cut it in into small pieces. Put the onion and oil in a large saucepan on medium heat. Cook for 3 minutes.

5 Add the bacon and fry for 6-7 minutes, stirring now and then, until the onion is soft and the bacon is turning brown.

6 Crush the garlic into the pan, then pour in the stock and tomatoes. Add the balsamic vinegar, sugar and mustard. Then, stir in the beans.

7 Heat the mixture until it boils, then turn down the heat so it bubbles gently. Put a lid on the pan, leaving a small gap.

8 Cook for 15 minutes. Turn off the heat and leave the beans to stand for a minute or two.

Other beans

Instead of navy beans you could use other types of canned beans such as white kidney beans, or even, for an inexpensive option, store-bought baked beans — wash off the sauce when you rinse them in step 1.

Beans with sausages

Extra ingredient: 12oz. - 1lb. package of sausages.
Cook the sausages according to the instructions on the package (broiling is healthiest). While they are cooking, make the beans, following steps 1-8. When the sausages are cooked, leave them to cool a little, then cut into bite-sized chunks. Stir them into the beans and cook for another 5 minutes.

Meat-free baked beans

For a vegetarian version, just leave out the bacon.

Spicy baked beans

Extra ingredients: 1 pinch of crushed red pepper or 1 teaspoon of chili powder. Follow steps 1-3, then add the pepper or chili to the pan when the bacon has around a minute left to cook. Follow the rest of the steps.

Nachos

Ingredients:

For the nachos:

6 yellow corn tortillas (gluten-free types are available)

4oz. hard cheese such as Cheddar or Monterey Jack (optional)

For the refried beans:

a 15oz. can of pinto beans, black beans or red kidney beans

1 small red onion

1½ tablespoons of olive oil

1 clove of garlic

1 teaspoon of ground cumin (optional)

1 pinch of crushed red pepper (optional)

For the guacamole:

2 ripe avocados

1 lime

1 clove of garlic

4 teaspoons of olive oil

a little hot pepper sauce (optional)

For the salsa:

3 ripe tomatoes

¼ red onion or ½ shallot

¼ lime

hot pepper sauce (optional)

Serves 4

Nachos are from Mexico. This version, with guacamole, salsa and refried beans, could be eaten as a snack or a light meal.

1 Make the guacamole, salsa and refried beans (see pages 27 and 51). Preheat the oven to 325°F.

2 Cut each tortilla into 6 wedges. Spread the wedges on two large cookie sheets.

3 Bake for 14-15 minutes, until they are golden-brown. Meanwhile, grate the cheese on the large holes of a grater.

4 When they are cooked, put the wedges from one cookie sheet on top of the wedges on the other one. Sprinkle the cheese on top.

5 Bake for 4-5 minutes, until the cheese has melted. Take out of the oven. Leave for 5 minutes to cool.

6 Meanwhile, put the refried beans on medium heat and stir for 5 minutes, to warm them up. Spoon all the toppings over the chips.

Bread & pastry

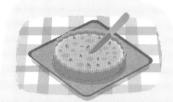

Recipes in other sections of this book use pastry too — from quiche (page 58) and feta cheese pies (page 52) to lemon curd tart (page 63).

Find out how to make your own bread and pizza crust.

About bread

Bread has been eaten all around the world for thousands of years. Here you can find some useful tips about how to cook it, and how to cook with it.

What is yeast?

Most bread is made from a dough made of wheat flour, water and yeast. When yeast becomes warm and moist, it gives off tiny bubbles of gas that make the dough rise. When the dough goes into the oven, it stops rising.

Bread flour

Bread is usually made with bread flour. When bread flour is pushed, squashed and stretched, it becomes stronger and stretchier than normal flour. This is called kneading (see the page opposite).

Flat breads

Some bread isn't made with yeast, so it stays flat. It often contains something other than yeast to make it rise — such as soda bread (page 45).

Leftover bread

Bread can go stale and hard pretty quickly. To keep it fresh for longer, store it in an airtight container or bag. However, stale bread is ideal for cooking, whether you're making summer fruit pudding (page 146) or just some toast.

This is dried rapid-rise yeast from a package.

This is what wheat looks like, before the grains are stripped off and ground up into flour.

Grains of wheat

This roll has risen, but it hasn't yet been cooked.

Bread flour

Kneading dough

1 When you're making bread, knead by pressing the heels of both hands, or your knuckles, into the dough. Then, push the dough away from you firmly.

2 Fold the dough in half and turn it around. Push the dough away from you again. Then, fold it in half and turn it around again.

3 Continue pushing the dough away from you, folding it and turning it, until it feels smooth and springy.

Leaving dough to rise

When you make bread, you need to leave it somewhere warm, such as a warm kitchen, or on a sunny windowsill (with the window closed). The warmth helps the yeast to make the dough rise quickly.

Cutting bread

1 To cut a loaf of bread into slices, you need a serrated knife. Hold the bread in one hand and the knife in the other.

2 Move the knife back and forth across the bread in a sawing movement. If the bread is very fresh, it's easier if you don't press down on it, and if you cut thick slices.

Making breadcrumbs

1 Use bread that's 2-3 days old. Cut off the crusts and tear the bread into pieces.

2 Put the bread in a food processor and pulse it until you get small breadcrumbs.

3 If you don't have a food processor, grate the bread on the big holes of a grater. If the bread feels too soft, you could toast it first.

Sandwiches

Ingredients:

2 slices of bread or one bread roll
  (you could use gluten-free bread)
butter, margarine or dairy-free spread
a filling, from the suggestions below

Makes 1 sandwich

Here you'll find instructions for different types of sandwiches. When you're making your sandwich, open out your pieces of bread like a book, then close them up again in the same way around the filling. This will help them to fit together better.

1 If you're using a roll, cut it in half and spread the cut sides with butter. If you're using bread, spread one side of each piece with butter.

2 Arrange the filling on one piece of roll or bread. Put the other piece on top. Press down gently. If you're using slices of bread, cut the sandwich into 2 or 4 pieces.

Cheese & coleslaw filling
You will need a few slices of your favorite cheese and around 2 tablespoons of coleslaw (see page 29).

Tuna mayonnaise filling
You will need around 2 tablespoons of tuna mayonnaise (see page 81).

BLT filling
You will need 2 slices of bacon, a few lettuce leaves and a medium-sized tomato. Broil the bacon (see page 89), tear up the lettuce leaves into small pieces and slice the tomato.

Cheese & cucumber filling
You will need 1 tablespoon of cream cheese and a piece of cucumber around 1½ inches long, sliced thinly.

Chicken & pesto filling
You will need half a cooked chicken breast (see page 89 for how to cook it), thinly sliced, and around a tablespoon of basil pesto (see page 68; pesto contains nuts).

Carrot & raisin filling
You will need around a tablespoon of carrot dip (page 26) and around a tablespoon of raisins.

Egg mayonnaise filling
You will need 1 hard boiled egg (see page 56) and 1 tablespoon of mayonnaise. Peel the egg, put it in a bowl, add the mayonnaise and mash with a fork.

Banana & chocolate filling
You will need half a ripe banana, sliced, and around a tablespoon of chocolate spread (may contain nuts).

Making a double decker sandwich

You will need 3 slices of bread, a little spread, and a double amount of filling. Butter each slice of bread on one side. Cover one slice with half the filling. Top with another slice, cover that with filling, then top with the final slice of bread. Then, cut up your sandwich.

Filling a wrap

1 Spread a filling on a soft flour tortilla or wrap. Leave a gap around the edge.

 2 Fold in the sides of the wrap.

3 Roll up the wrap from the bottom. Then, cut it in half.

Making pita pockets

1 Toast a pita pocket bread in a toaster.

 2 Let it cool for a minute or two. Then, cut it in half.

3 Open up the halves into pockets, using your fingers. Then, spoon in a filling.

Making an open sandwich

Butter 1 slice of bread, then arrange the filling on top. It's easiest to eat open sandwiches with a knife and fork.

Toast toppings

Ingredients:

4 tablespoons of raw sugar
or brown sugar

1 teaspoon of ground cinnamon

4 large or 8 small slices of bread
(you could use gluten-free bread)

a little butter, margarine or
dairy-free spread

Serves 4

Hot toast spread with butter or jam is a treat in itself, but these toppings make it extra special. The main recipe is for toast topped with crunchy cinnamon sugar. You'll find suggestions for other toppings on the opposite page.

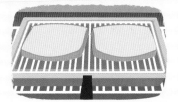

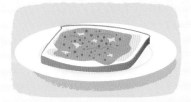

1 Put the sugar and cinnamon in a small bowl and mix them together. Then, turn the broiler to medium and leave it to heat up for 5 minutes.

2 Arrange the bread in the broiler pan and position it around 2 inches away from the heat. Broil for 1-2 minutes, until the bread is toasted.

3 Turn the pieces of bread over and spread the un-toasted sides with butter or spread. Sprinkle over the cinnamon sugar and put the bread back under the broiler.

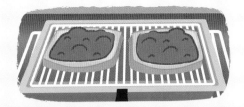

4 Broil the bread for 1-2 minutes, until the sugar is bubbling. Then, leave the toast in the broiler pan to cool for 5 minutes, as the sugar will be extremely hot.

5 When the toast has cooled, you could press cookie cutters into it, to cut it into shapes. Eat them with some fresh fruit, if you like.

Cheesy toast

You will need a small bunch of fresh chives, 1 large egg, 1¾ cups grated hard cheese such as Cheddar or Monterey Jack, 2 tablespoons softened butter, ½ teaspoon of mustard (optional) and 4 large or 8 small slices of bread (or gluten-free bread).

Snip up the chives. Break the egg into a bowl. Beat it with a fork. Add the chives, cheese, butter and mustard and mix. Heat the broiler, follow step 2, then turn the bread over, spread the cheese mixture to the edges and broil for 1-2 minutes, until the cheese is bubbling. Cut up with cookie cutters, if you like.

Banana toast

You will need 2 ripe bananas, 4 large or 8 small slices of bread (or gluten-free bread) and some honey or chocolate spread (may contain nuts) or peanut butter (contains nuts).

Cut the banana into thick slices. Toast the bread in a toaster or toast both sides under the broiler. Spread one side of each slice of toast with your chosen topping, then arrange the slices of banana on top.

Toast shapes like these are pretty for a party, but eat the scraps, too.

Homemade bread

Ingredients:

3 cups bread flour

1 teaspoon of salt

2 teaspoons of dried rapid rise yeast
    (1 package)

1 cup warm water

2 tablespoons of olive or vegetable oil

Makes 1 loaf or 12 rolls

There's nothing like homemade bread, fresh from the oven. It's not difficult to make: you just need to leave some time for the dough to rise.

When you make the dough, the water you add should feel really warm when you put your hand in it. But make sure it's not too hot, or the bread won't rise properly.

1 Sift the flour and salt into a large mixing bowl. Add the yeast and stir it in. Put the water in a measuring cup, add the oil, then pour them into the bowl.

2 Stir until everything comes together. Put the dough on a surface dusted with flour and knead it for 10 minutes (see page 135), or until it is smooth and springy.

3 If you're in a hurry, skip to step 5. If you're not, put the dough in a clean bowl, cover it with a clean dishtowel and leave it in a warm place to rise.

4 After around 1½-2 hours, the dough should have doubled in size. Put it back on the floury surface. Gently squeeze and press it to squash out the tiny air bubbles.

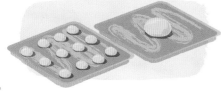

5 Shape the dough into one large ball or 12 small balls and put on a greased cookie sheet. Cover with a clean dishtowel and leave in a warm place to rise.

6 Wait until the dough has doubled in size. If you followed steps 3-4, this will take around 40 minutes; if you didn't, it will take around 1½-2 hours. Then preheat the oven to 425°F.

You could decorate the top of your bread with seeds.

7 Brush the dough with a little milk (optional), then put the bread in the oven. For one loaf, bake for 30 minutes. For rolls, bake for 12-15 minutes.

8 The bread is cooked when the crust is brown and it sounds hollow when you tap the bottom. If it's not cooked, bake for 10 minutes more and test again. When it's cooked, put it on a wire rack to cool.

Whole-wheat bread

This recipe also works if you use whole-wheat bread flour, or a mixture of half regular bread flour and half whole-wheat bread flour.

Seeded bread

For seeded bread, stir 3 tablespoons of poppy seeds, sesame seeds or sunflower seeds into the flour at step 1. Sprinkle an extra tablespoon of seeds over the bread at step 5. (Seeds may not be suitable for those with nut allergies.)

Other bread ideas

Homemade bread tastes delicious spread with a little butter, jam or lemon curd (page 62), or with soup, baked beans or scrambled eggs (pages 30, 130 and 57). You could also use it in the other recipes in this section, such as summer pudding (page 146).

Pizza

Ingredients:

For the crust:

1¼ cups bread flour

¼ teaspoon of salt

¾ teaspoon of rapid rise yeast

½ cup warm water

2 teaspoons of olive oil

For the tomato sauce:

2 cloves of garlic

1 tablespoon of olive oil

a 15oz. can of diced tomatoes

2 tablespoons of tomato paste

1 pinch of sugar

½ teaspoon of dried oregano

For the toppings:

1 cup grated cheese such as mozzarella
   or Cheddar (optional)

any other toppings you like, such as

   black olives

   sliced mushrooms

   strips of ham

   arugula or basil leaves

   thinly sliced red bell peppers

   sliced tomatoes

Serves 4

1 To mix and knead the bread
dough for the pizza crust, follow
steps 1-2 in the recipe for
homemade bread on page 140.

Pizzas were first made in the Italian city of Naples more than a hundred years ago. This recipe makes enough pizza dough for one deep, puffy pizza, or two thin and crispy ones. Once you've made the pizza crust and the tomato sauce, you can add all your favorite toppings (see opposite for some suggestions).

If you're in a hurry, don't leave the dough to rise.

2 Put the dough in a clean bowl, cover it with a dishtowel and leave it in a warm place. Then make the tomato sauce following steps 1-2 on page 32. Add the oregano at step 1.

3 After around 1½-2 hours, the dough should have doubled in size. Put it back on the floury surface. Gently squeeze and press it to squash out the tiny air bubbles.

4 Preheat the oven to 400°F. Use a paper towel to wipe a little oil over a large cookie sheet (or, for 2 pizzas, 2 large cookie sheets).

You can roll the dough into a circle, or a rectangle, like this.

5 If you're making two thin pizzas, divide the dough into two pieces. Roll out your dough with a rolling pin until it is around 12 inches across. For two thin pizzas, do this twice.

Spread the sauce with the back of a spoon.

6 If you're making two pizzas, divide the sauce between the crusts. If you're making one pizza, put on half the tomato sauce (save the rest for another day). Spread out the sauce, leaving a gap around the edge.

7 Scatter around half the cheese over the tomato sauce. Then, add your other toppings and scatter the rest of the cheese over the top.

Pizza toppings

Here are some ideas for toppings:

o grated cheese with ham and sliced mushrooms

o sliced pepperoni, black olives and grated cheese

o sliced soft mozzarella cheese, sliced tomatoes and fresh basil leaves

o four different types of cheese

o sliced onion and red bell pepper with feta cheese

o anchovies or drained canned tuna with sliced red onion and black olives

8 Bake for around 20 minutes, until the dough is golden brown and the cheese is bubbling. You could scatter over some fresh arugula leaves, if you like. Cut your pizza or pizzas into slices with a sharp knife.

Cinnamon rolls

Ingredients:

2¼ cups bread flour

2 teaspoons rapid rise yeast (1 package)

1 tablespoon of sugar

½ teaspoon of salt

⅓ cup + 1 tablespoon milk

½ stick (¼ cup) butter

1 large egg

¼ cup (packed) dark brown sugar

1½ teaspoons of ground cinnamon

1 tablespoon of honey or maple syrup

You will also need a 9 inch square cake pan that's at least 2½ inches deep.

Makes 9 rolls

These sweet, sticky rolls are made using bread dough spread with cinnamon sugar, rolled up into a spiral and cut into pieces. You'll also find a version made with pecans on the page opposite.

1 First, line the pan with parchment paper (see page 161).

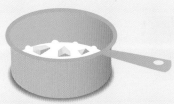

2 Put the flour in a large bowl. Stir in the yeast, sugar and salt.

3 Put the milk and half the butter in a saucepan. Put the pan on low heat, until the butter melts. Turn off the heat.

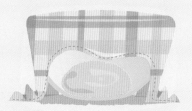

4 Break the egg into a cup and beat it with a fork. Add the egg and the milk mixture to the flour mixture and stir until it comes together in a ball.

5 Put the dough on a clean surface dusted with flour. Knead it for 10 minutes (see page 135), until it feels smooth and springy.

6 If you're in a hurry, skip to step 8. If you're not, put the dough in a clean bowl. Cover it with a clean dishtowel and leave it in a warm place to rise.

7 After around 1½-2 hours, the dough should have doubled in size. Put it back on the floury surface. Gently squeeze it to squash out the tiny air bubbles.

8 Put the remaining butter in a saucepan on low heat. When the butter melts, take the pan off the heat and stir in the brown sugar and cinnamon.

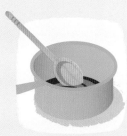

9 Roll the dough into a rectangle around 8 inches x 15 inches. Spread the buttery mixture over it, leaving the edges bare. Roll it up from one of the long ends into a sausage shape.

10 Cut across the roll to make 9 equal-sized pieces. Arrange them in the pan in 3 rows of 3, then cover with a dishtowel and leave in a warm place to rise.

11 Wait until the rolls have doubled in size. If you followed steps 6-7, this will take around 40 minutes; if you didn't, it will take around 1½-2 hours.

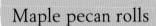

12 Preheat the oven to 425°F. Take off the dishtowel and put the pan in the oven for 20-25 minutes or until the rolls are golden-brown.

13 Leave the rolls to cool for 15 minutes. Then, turn the pan upside down over a wire rack and shake so the rolls pop out. Turn them over. Brush them with the honey or maple syrup.

Maple pecan rolls

Extra ingredients: ⅔ cup chopped pecans. Use maple syrup instead of honey. Follow steps 1-8 of the main recipe. At step 9, sprinkle the chopped pecans over the dough just before you roll it up. Then, follow steps 10-13, brushing on the syrup instead of the honey. Contains nuts.

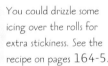

You could drizzle some icing over the rolls for extra stickiness. See the recipe on pages 164-5.

Little summer puddings

Ingredients:

700g (1lb 8oz) summer berries
such as strawberries, redcurrants,
raspberries & blueberries

125g (4½oz) caster sugar

12 slices of white bread,
at least a day old

You will also need:

4 small dishes, such as ramekins
or teacups

a mug or glass with a rim
around the same size as the
bottom of your dishes

4 small, full food cans or jam
jars, to use as weights.

Serves 4

It's best to use good
quality or home-made
bread for this recipe.
Cheap, sliced bread may
go a bit slimy.

Summer pudding is made with ripe summer berries and
leftover bread. The bread soaks up the fruit juices and goes
deliciously pink, sweet and soft. This recipe is for 4 individual
puddings, but you could make one big one, using a 1 litre
(2 pint) pudding basin. Slice it into wedges, like a cake.

Stir every
now and
then.

1 Rinse and drain the fruit. Pull the
stalks and leaves out of the strawberries.
Cut up any large strawberries. Pull any
currants off their stems, using a fork.

2 Put the fruit, sugar and 2
tablespoons of water in a pan. Cook
over a low heat for 5 minutes, until
the sugar has dissolved.

3 Turn up the heat so the mixture
bubbles gently for 2-3 minutes.
When the fruit is soft, but not
mushy, spoon it into a bowl, leaving
the juice in the pan.

4 Use the rim of the mug or glass
like a cutter, to stamp out 4 circles
from 4 slices of bread. Cut the
crusts off the rest of the bread and
cut the bread into wide strips.

6 Fill any gaps
between the strips
with small pieces of
bread. Then, line the
other dishes in the
same way.

5 Dip one side of a bread circle in the fruit juice. Place the circle in
the bottom of a dish, juice-side down. Dip the strips too, and overlap
them to line the sides of the dish. Put them juice-side out, too.

7 Spoon the fruit and juices into the lined dishes. Trim off any bread that's sticking up. Put more bread strips over the fruit.

8 Put some food wrap loosely over each dish. Put the dishes on a baking tray and put it in the fridge.

9 Put a full food can or jam jar on top of each one. Leave for at least 4 hours. Then, remove the weights and food wrap.

Run a knife around each pudding first.

10 Turn each dish upside down over a plate. The pudding should pop out.

Autumn puddings

For autumn puddings, replace the summer berries with blackberries, sliced plums, and peeled and chopped apples and pears. Cook them for a few minutes longer, to make sure they are soft.

About pastry

Pastry is usually made from flour, butter and a little water or milk. It can be crisp, flaky, puffy or soft, and it goes equally well with sweet or savory fillings. Here you can find some tips about making and using pastry.

Different types

The recipes in this section show you how to make shortcrust pastry and choux pastry. But you can buy many types of pastry dough ready-made, either chilled or frozen. It comes in sheets, or blocks that you need to roll out.

Resting dough

When you make pastry dough, or roll it out, you sometimes need to leave it in the refrigerator for a little while before you cook it. This is called 'resting' the dough. It stops it from shrinking too much when you put it in the oven.

Ceramic beans, like these, or dried beans, are used to weigh pastry dough down during blind baking.

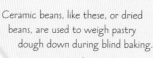

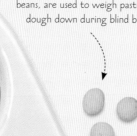

Blind baking

When you make a pastry crust for a tart or quiche, you need to bake it on its own first. This is called 'blind baking' — see steps 2–3 on page 58.

Rubbing in

1 When you make shortcrust dough (page 152), you rub the butter into the flour. It's a good idea to stir the chunks of butter into the flour first.

2 Use the tips of your fingers and thumbs to pick up some butter and flour. Squash and rub them together so they start to mix. Lift the mixture up and let it drop back into the bowl as you rub.

3 Continue rubbing. The lumps of butter will become smaller and smaller. Stop when they are the same size as small breadcrumbs.

Rolling out

1 Sprinkle some flour on a clean surface and on a rolling pin. Put the dough on the surface.

2 Roll the rolling pin over the dough once, then turn the dough a quarter of the way around on the surface.

3 Roll and turn the dough again and again in the same way. Continue until the dough is the size or thickness you need for the recipe.

Lining a pan or dish

1 First, wipe a little softened butter or oil over the insides of the pan, using a paper towel. Then, roll the dough around the rolling pin.

3 Trim off the edges using scissors, but don't cut too close to the pan. Then, cover the dough with plastic food wrap and put the pan in the refrigerator for 20 minutes.

2 Lift up the rolling pin and unroll the dough over the pan. Gently push the dough into the hollow of the pan.

Tomato tarts

Ingredients:

1 large red onion

1 sheet of store-bought puff
pastry dough

2 tablespoons of milk

½ cup full-fat cream cheese

1 tablespoon of olive oil

8oz. ripe tomatoes

½ teaspoon of Italian herb blend

Makes 6 tarts

This recipe uses a sheet of store-bought puff pastry dough as a crust for light vegetable tarts. The main recipe is for tomato tarts, but the instructions opposite show you how to make other types, too.

1 Preheat the oven to 425°F. Wipe some cooking oil over a cookie sheet using a paper towel. Take the pastry and cream cheese out of the refrigerator.

2 Cut the onion into thin slices. Put the olive oil and onion in a frying pan on gentle heat. Cook for 10 minutes, stirring every now and then, until the onion is soft.

3 While the onions are cooking, unwrap and unroll the pastry and put it on the cookie sheet. Cut the pastry into 6 pieces.

4 Mix 1 tablespoon of the milk into the cream cheese. Spread the cheese over the pastry, leaving a 1 inch border at the edge. Brush the remaining milk onto the border.

5 If the tomatoes are big, cut them into slices. If they are small (cherry) tomatoes, cut them in half. Arrange them over the cream cheese. Don't cover the milky border.

6 When the onions are cooked, stir in the herbs and a pinch of salt and pepper. Spoon the onions over the tomatoes.

7 Bake for around 15-20 minutes, until the pastry is risen and golden brown. Leave the tarts on the cookie sheet for 3 minutes to cool a little. You could scatter some fresh herbs over the top.

Mushroom tarts

Replace the tomatoes with 8oz baby Bella mushrooms and 1 tablespoon of butter. Follow step 1. Wipe the mushrooms and cut them into slices. At step 2, cook the onions for 5 minutes, add the mushrooms and butter and cook for 5 more minutes. Follow steps 3-5. Arrange the mushrooms over the cream cheese and follow step 7.

Red bell pepper tarts

Replace the tomatoes with 2 red or yellow bell peppers. Follow step 1. Cut the tops off the bell peppers. Cut the bell peppers in half, pull out the seeds and white pith and cut the bell peppers into slices as thick as a pencil. At step 2, cook the onions for 5 minutes, add the peppers and cook for 5 more minutes. Follow steps 3-5. Then, arrange the peppers over the cream cheese and follow step 7.

Shortcrust pastry dough

Ingredients:

1½ cups all-purpose flour

¾ stick (6 tablespoons) chilled butter

2 tablespoons of cold water

Makes 12 small tart shells or 1 large pie crust

Good shortcrust pastry is light and crisp, and can be used in all kinds of dishes, both sweet and savory. It's easy to make, but it's best if you don't squash or press the dough too hard. The more gently you treat the dough, the lighter it will be.

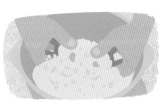

1 Sift the flour into a large bowl. Cut the butter into chunks and put them in the bowl. Mix the butter around with your hands to coat it with flour.

2 Use the tips of your fingers and thumbs to pick up some butter and flour, and squash and rub them together so they start to mix. Lift the mixture up and let it drop back into the bowl as you rub.

3 Continue rubbing. The lumps of butter will become smaller. Stop when they are the same size as small breadcrumbs.

4 Add the cold water. Stir it in using a blunt knife, until everything starts to stick together. Add another teaspoon or two of water if it feels too dry.

5 Pat the pastry dough into a ball and press gently to flatten it. Then, cover it with plastic food wrap and refrigerate for 20 minutes. This will make it easier to roll out.

6 Next, sprinkle some flour onto a clean work surface and a rolling pin. Unwrap the pastry dough and put it on the floury surface.

7 Roll out the pastry dough until it is slightly bigger than the pan you need to line, or around half as thick as a pencil.

Pear & berry pies

For the dough you will need 1 cup all-purpose flour, ½ stick (¼ cup) chilled butter and 1½-2 tablespoons of cold water. For the filling you will need a 14oz. can of pear halves, 1¾ cups fresh or frozen blueberries and 1 tablespoon of sugar. You will also need 4 individual ovenproof dishes.

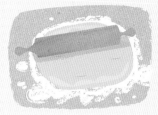

1 Follow steps 1-7 of the main recipe to make the pastry dough and roll it out until it is half as thick as a pencil. Preheat the oven to 400°F.

Instead of blueberries, you could use the same amount of fresh or frozen raspberries or blackberries, or a mixture of different berries. The berries will make the pear turn a pinkish-purple color.

2 Prepare the filling by following the note about quick fruit crisp on page 17. Divide the filling between the dishes. Cut the pastry dough into strips around 1 inch wide.

3 Brush some water around the edge of the dishes. Lay some strips over each dish, then lay some more strips across them, in a criss-cross pattern.

4 Press the strips onto the edges of the dishes and trim off any excess. Bake for 25-30 minutes, until the crust is golden brown.

Little fruit pies

Ingredients:

For the dough:

1½ cups all-purpose flour

¾ stick (6 tablespoons) chilled butter

2½ tablespoons of cold water

For the filling:

5 tablespoons of raspberry jam
or apricot preserves or lemon curd

For the fruit topping:

around 2½ cups fresh berries such as
raspberries, blueberries, redcurrants
and strawberries

For the glaze (optional):

5 tablespoon of raspberry jam
or apricot preserves

1 tablespoon of lemon juice

You will also need:

a 12-cup muffin pan

a 3 inch round or fluted
cookie cutter

Makes 12

This recipe shows how to use shortcrust pastry dough to make mini pies. You can fill them with fresh fruits and then brush on a shiny glaze.

1 Follow steps 1-7 on page 152 to make the pastry dough. While it's in the refrigerator, preheat on the oven to 400°F. Use a paper towel to wipe a little softened butter into the cups of the muffin pan.

2 Roll out the dough by following the steps on page 149. Use the cookie cutter to cut out lots of circles.

3 Put one circle over each cup in the muffin pan. Dip your finger in some flour and use it to push the circles gently into the cups.

4 Roll the scraps of dough into a ball, roll it out again and cut more circles, until you have filled the pan.

5 Spoon one teaspoon of jam or preserves into each cup. Put the pan in the oven for 10-12 minutes, until the crust is golden.

6 Take the pan out of the oven. The jam or preserves or curd will be very hot. Leave to cool for a few minutes, then lift the pies out of the pan. Put them on a wire rack. Leave them to cool completely.

7 To fill your tarts with fruits, wash the berries in a strainer under cold running water, then pat them dry with a clean dishtowel.

8 Pull the green stems and leaves out of the strawberries. Cut any large strawberries into pieces.

9 To make a glaze for your tarts, put the jam or preserves into a small bowl and add the lemon juice. Mix them together.

10 Pile all the berries into the tarts, then brush the glaze over the berries to make them look shiny.

Large fruit pie

You could make one large pie, using an 8 inch pie pan. Follow steps 1-7 on page 152 to make the dough and the steps on page 149 to line the dish. Spoon 5 tablespoons of jam or preserves into the pie crust. Spread it out with the back of a spoon. Bake for around 20 minutes, until the crust is golden. Follow steps 7-10 of the main recipe here, to fill your pie with berries and add a glaze.

Cream puffs

Ingredients:

For the pastry puffs:

½ cup all-purpose flour

2 large eggs

4 tablespoons of butter

½ cup water

For the filling:

2 oranges

¾ cup heavy or whipping cream

2 tablespoons of powdered sugar

Makes around 15

Cream puffs are made with a type of pastry called choux pastry. In this recipe the pastry puffs are filled with oranges and cream. You could drizzle them with caramel sauce – see the recipe on the page opposite.

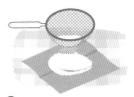

1 Preheat the oven to 425°F. Use a paper towel to wipe some butter over two cookie sheets. Hold each cookie sheet briefly under cold running water, then shake off the water.

2 Cut a large rectangle of parchment paper, fold it in half, then unfold it again. Sift the flour onto it. Then, break the eggs into a cup and beat them with a fork.

3 Cut the butter into small chunks and put them in a saucepan with the water. Heat gently. As soon as the mixture boils, take it off the heat. Right away, fold up the parchment paper and pour all the flour into the pan.

4 Quickly beat in the flour. Continue beating for around a minute, until the mixture starts to come away from the sides of the pan and form a ball in the middle. Then, leave it to cool for 5 minutes.

5 Add a tablespoon of the egg to the mixture and beat it in well. Do this again and again until all the egg is added. Put heaped teaspoons of the mixture on the cookie sheets, one by one, spacing them well apart.

6 Bake for 10 minutes. Then, turn down the heat to 375°F. Bake for another 10-12 minutes until the pastry puffs are raised and dark golden.

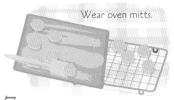

Wear oven mitts.

7 Use a spatula to move the puffs to a wire rack, to cool. Make a hole in the side of each puff with a sharp knife, to let out any steam.

8 While the puffs are cooling, make the filling. Grate the zest from the oranges, using the small holes of a grater. Put it in a large mixing bowl.

9 Cut the oranges into slices around as thick as your little finger. Cut the skin off the slices, like this. Then, cut the slices into small pieces.

10 Pour the cream into the bowl. Sift in the powdered sugar. Whip the cream with a whisk or electric mixer until it is very thick (see page 41).

11 Try lifting up the whisk – if the cream stays in a floppy point, like this, you have whipped it enough. Add the orange pieces and mix them in gently, using a metal spoon.

12 Cut the puffs in half. Spoon some cream and fruit into the bottom half of each puff, then put the top back on.

Caramel sauce

You will need 2 tablespoons butter, ¼ cup (packed) dark brown sugar and ⅔ cup heavy or whipping cream.

Put the butter and sugar in a saucepan on low heat. Stir until the sugar has dissolved and you have a smooth paste. Stir in the cream. Let it bubble gently for 2 minutes. Leave to cool for 10 minutes, then drizzle over the cream puffs.

Puff pastry spirals

Ingredients:

1 sheet of store-bought puff
  pastry dough

4 tablespoons of basil pesto, store-bought or
  homemade (see page 68); contains nuts

2oz. hard cheese such as Cheddar or
  Parmesan (⅓ cup when grated)

Makes around 40

Tomato spirals

To make nut-free,
tomato spirals, replace
the pesto with 4
tablespoons of sun-dried
tomato paste from
a tube or jar.

You can flavor these little snacks using basil pesto or
sun-dried tomato paste.

1 Unroll the pastry dough.
Cut it into three equal-sized
strips, like this.

2 Divide the basil pesto between the strips.
Use a blunt knife to spread it out, leaving a
thin border around the edge of each strip.

3 Brush some water along one edge of each strip, then roll up
the dough from the opposite edge. Wrap the rolls in plastic food
wrap and put them in the freezer for 30 minutes.

4 Use a paper towel to wipe a little
oil over two cookie sheets. Preheat
your oven to 400°F.
Grate the cheese on
the small holes of a
grater, if necessary.

5 After 30 minutes, take the rolls
out of the freezer and unwrap them.
Cut them into slices ½ inch wide.
Arrange the slices on the cookie sheets,
spaced apart. Sprinkle over the cheese.

6 Bake for 10-12 minutes,
until the spirals are puffy and
golden. Take them out of the
oven. After 5 minutes, put the
spirals on a wire rack to cool.

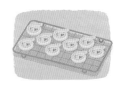

Cookies & cakes

As well as the cakes in this section, you'll also find recipes for different types of cheesecakes on pages 54-55.

These spice cookies are cut out using cookie cutters and decorated with icing or powdered sugar.

About cookies

This section contains recipes for cookies and bars. They are easier to make than cakes, so this is a good place to start if you're new to baking. Here are some useful tips to help you.

Measuring

When you're baking, measure the ingredients accurately, or your baking might not turn out right.

Cutting out

When you cut shapes from dough, you'll have lots of scraps left. Squeeze them together, roll them out and cut more shapes.

Sifting

Sometimes you need to sift ingredients. Hold the strainer or sifter slightly above a bowl and shake it gently, so the ingredients fall through. If there are lumps (for example, of powdered sugar), squash them through with the back of a spoon.

Storing cookies

Keep your finished cookies in an airtight container. All the cookie recipes in this section will keep for at least a few days this way.

Greasing a pan or cookie sheet

1 Use a paper towel to scoop up a little softened butter or a little cooking oil.

2 Wipe the paper towel over the pan or cookie sheet, so it's thinly covered.

Lining a pan or cookie sheet

1 Put the pan or cookie sheet on some parchment paper. Draw around it.

2 Cut out the shape, cutting just inside the line.

3 Wipe a little butter or oil over the pan or cookie sheet.

4 Put in the parchment paper shape.

Beating butter & sugar

Put the sugar and softened butter in a large mixing bowl. Stir them together with a wooden spoon. Then, beat them quickly with the spoon, until you have a smooth, fluffy mixture.

Tip:

If the butter is hard to beat, pour hot water into another bowl, dry it, then transfer the mixture to it.

Melting chocolate

1 Fill a saucepan a quarter full of water. Heat until the water bubbles. Turn off the heat.

2 Put the chocolate in a heat-proof bowl that fits the pan. The bottom of the bowl shouldn't touch the bottom of the pan.

3 Carefully, put the bowl in the pan. Leave it until the chocolate has melted.

Drizzling

Scoop up some icing or melted chocolate on a small spoon. Tip the spoon so a little of the mixture slides off onto a cookie. Move the spoon across the cookie, leaving a trail of the mixture.

Chocolate granola bars

Ingredients:

1 cup + 2 tablespoons semisweet
   chocolate chips

7 tablespoons butter, margarine or
   dairy-free spread

1 tablespoon of corn syrup

1 cup granola (or gluten-free granola)

¼ cup candied cherries

⅓ cup raisins or golden raisins

½ cup unsalted, shelled nuts (optional)

You will also need:

a cake pan or plastic container around
   7 inches wide

a heatproof bowl that fits into
   your saucepan

Makes around 12

These delicious chocolaty bars are full of granola, fruit and nuts. You don't have to bake them in the oven – all you have to do is melt the butter and chocolate, stir in the other ingredients and put everything in the refrigerator to set.

1 Line the cake pan or plastic container with parchment paper (see page 161).

2 Fill the saucepan a quarter full of cold water. Put the pan on medium heat, until the water is just bubbling. Turn off the heat.

3 Put the chocolate chips in the heatproof bowl. Put the butter or spread and corn syrup in too.

4 Wearing oven mitts, put the bowl in the pan. Leave it for 5 minutes, then stir until the butter and chocolate have melted. Then, still wearing oven mitts, take the bowl out of the pan.

5 Put the granola, candied cherries, raisins and nuts in the bowl. Stir to coat them in the chocolate mixture.

6 Scrape the mixture into the prepared pan or box. Refrigerate for at least 1 hour to set.

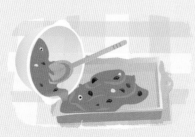

7 Run a knife around the pan, then turn it out onto a plate or board (see page 171). Cut it up into lots of small bars. Store in the refrigerator.

Nut-free granola bars

If you prefer to leave out the nuts, use nut-free granola and replace the almonds or other nuts with ½ cup extra granola or ⅓ cup extra raisins.

Cereal bars

If you like, you could replace the granola with 2 cups of other types of breakfast cereal, such as cornflakes or crispy rice cereal.

Other fruit & nuts

You could replace the fruit and nuts with the same amount of...

o chopped dried apricots, dates, figs or mango
o chopped candied pineapple
o unsalted peanuts or pistachio nuts
o hazelnuts, pecans, walnuts or macadamia nuts

Drizzled granola bars

To make your bars look like the ones here, melt ⅓ cup white chocolate chips following the steps on page 161. Find out how to drizzle it on page 161, too.

163

Spice cookies

Ingredients:

For the cookies:

1 ¾ cups +2 tablespoons
self-rising flour

2 ½ teaspoons of ground cinnamon

1 teaspoon of ground ginger

½ teaspoon of apple pie spice

½ stick (¼ cup) butter

¼ cup (packed) dark brown sugar

3 ½ tablespoons of corn syrup
or honey

For the icing:

1 cup + 3 tablespoons powdered sugar

You will also need some cookie
cutters of any shape

Makes around 20

You could drizzle patterns
like these onto your
finished cookies.

These crisp, cut-out cookies have a nice, sugary, spicy flavor. If you don't have any cookie cutters, use the rim of a small glass or cup to cut them out. You can ice your finished cookies, but they taste good just as they are, or with a little powdered sugar sifted over them.

1 Preheat the oven to 350°F. Line 2 cookie sheets with parchment paper (see page 161).

2 Sift the flour, cinnamon, ginger and apple pie spice into a large bowl. Put the butter, sugar and syrup or honey in a saucepan. Heat gently, stirring now and then, until the butter has melted.

3 Take the pan off the heat, add the flour and mix, until the mixture clings together. Put a lid on the pan and leave the dough for around 10 minutes, to become cool and firm.

4 Put the dough on a clean surface sprinkled with flour. Knead it gently for a couple of minutes until it is smooth. Divide the dough in half and put one half back in the pan, with the lid on.

5 Roll out the piece of dough until it is half as thick as a pencil. Use cutters to cut out lots of cookies and put them on the cookie sheets. Roll out the other piece of dough and cut out more cookies.

6 Squeeze all the scraps of dough together, then roll them out again to make more cookies. Bake the cookies for 8-10 minutes, until they are golden brown.

7 Leave the cookies on the cookie sheets for 2 minutes, then put them on a wire rack to cool. Meanwhile, make the icing.

8 Sift the powdered sugar into a bowl. Stir in 2 ½ tablespoons of warm water to make a smooth paste. Spread or drizzle it onto the cold cookies using a small spoon.

Chocolate chip cookies

Ingredients:

6 tablespoons of butter, softened

7 tablespoons of sugar

1/3 cup light brown sugar

1 large egg

1 teaspoon of vanilla extract
(optional)

1½ cups all-purpose flour

½ teaspoon of baking powder

1/3 cup milk or semisweet chocolate
chips, or candy-coated chocolates

Makes around 24

These classic vanilla cookies stay soft in the middle, so they're slightly chewy when you bite into them. You can make them with any type of chocolate chips: semisweet, milk or white. For colorful cookies with extra crunch, use candy-coated chocolates.

1 Preheat the oven to 350°F. Use a paper towel to wipe a little cooking oil over two cookie sheets.

2 Put the butter and both types of sugar in a large mixing bowl. Stir them together with a wooden spoon, then beat them very quickly, until you have a smooth, creamy mixture.

3 Break the egg into a cup and beat it with a fork. Put the vanilla extract in too and mix it in.

Double chocolate cookies

Extra ingredient: ¼ cup unsweetened cocoa powder. Follow steps 1-4. At step 5, use just 1¼ cups of flour and sift the cocoa powder into the bowl at the same time. Then, follow steps 6-7 as normal.

4 Put a little of the egg mixture in the large bowl, and mix it in well. Continue adding the egg mixture a little at a time until it is all used up. Stir well each time.

5 Sift the flour and baking powder into the bowl. Stir the mixture until it is smooth. Add the chocolate chips or candy coated chocolates and stir them in.

6 Take a heaped teaspoon of the mixture and use your hands to roll it into a ball. Put it on the cookie sheet and flatten it slightly. Do the same with the rest of the mixture.

7 Bake for 10 minutes, until the cookies have spread and look slightly browned and cracked. Leave on the cookie sheets for a few minutes. Then, put on a wire rack to cool.

Fruity cookies

Instead of the chocolate, add ¾ cup of any of the following ingredients:

o raisins or golden raisins
o dried cranberries or cherries
o chopped dates, figs or dried apricots

Chocolate & nut cookies

You could use just ½ cup chocolate chips, plus ¾ cup of any of these ingredients:

o chopped hazelnuts, walnuts or pecans
o unsalted peanuts or pistachio nuts
o chopped macadamia nuts or brazil nuts

Oatmeal raisin cookies

Ingredients:

1 orange

½ cup raisins

¾ cup all-purpose flour

¾ cup old-fashioned (rolled) oats

½ teaspoon of baking powder

½ stick (¼ cup) chilled butter

6 tablespoons light brown sugar

1 large egg

Makes around 20

These sweet oatmeal cookies look rough and chunky, but they're deliciously moist and chewy. In this recipe you mix the butter and flour by rubbing them between the tips of your fingers and thumbs. This is the same method used in making pastry dough (see page 149).

1 Preheat the oven to 350°F. Use a paper towel to wipe a little cooking oil over two cookie sheets.

2 Grate the zest from the orange. Try not to grate any of the white pith underneath. Put the zest in a small bowl.

To shape these cookies, you drop teaspoons of the mixture onto cookie sheets. Cookies made in this way are sometimes called 'drop cookies'.

3 Cut the orange in half and squeeze the juice from one half. Add 1 tablespoon of the juice to the zest. Put the raisins in too.

4 Put the flour, oats and baking powder in a large bowl. Cut the butter into chunks and put them in too. Use your fingertips to rub the butter into the flour mixture, until it looks like small breadcrumbs.

5 Add the sugar to the flour mixture and stir it in. Break the egg into a cup and beat it with a fork. Pour the egg, raisins, zest and juice into the large bowl.

6 Stir everything together. Take heaped teaspoonfuls of the mixture and drop them onto the cookie sheets, spacing them well apart. Put the cookie sheets in the oven.

7 Bake for 12-15 minutes, until the cookies are golden brown. Take them out of the oven and leave them for a few minutes. Then put them on a wire rack to cool.

Oatmeal, apricot & almond cookies

Replace the raisins with ¼ cup chopped dried apricots and ½ cup chopped almonds.

Follow steps 1-3, using the apricots instead of the raisins. Follow step 4. At step 5, add the apricots instead of the raisins, add the almonds, then follow steps 6 and 7. Contains nuts.

Oatmeal & seed cookies

Extra ingredients: 4 tablespoons of sesame seeds and 4 tablespoons of sunflower seeds. Follow steps 1-2. At step 3, use just ⅓ cup raisins. Follow steps 4 and 5. Add the seeds. Follow steps 6 and 7. Seeds may not be suitable for those with nut allergies.

Oatmeal, lemon & white chocolate cookies

Replace the orange and raisins with 1 lemon and ½ cup white chocolate chips.

Follow step 1. In steps 2-3, replace the lemon with the orange. Follow steps 4-5, add the chocolate chips and follow steps 6-7.

About cakes

Cakes aren't difficult to make, as long as you follow a few simple rules. You'll find them here, along with tips that should help you to bake a perfect cake every time.

Measuring

Measure all the ingredients for your cakes as accurately as you can, or the recipe might not turn out exactly right.

When is it cooked?

To check if a cake is cooked, carefully poke the middle of the cake gently with a finger. It should feel firm and springy. If it doesn't, cook for 5-10 minutes more and then test it again.

Pan sizes

Keep to the size and shape of pan the recipe says, or the cake might not turn out right.

Greasing and lining pans

See page 161 for how to do this.

Keep the oven closed

Don't keep opening the oven door to check on your cake. Set a timer for as long as the recipe says and only open the door when it rings — unless you think something is burning.

Storing cakes

Most of the cakes in this section will keep in an airtight container for a few days. And if you put cream or fresh fruit on or in a cake, it's best to put the container in the refrigerator.

You can make allergy-free cakes — see page 178.

Adding eggs

When you mix eggs into a cake mixture, you usually have to add them a little at a time. If you add them all at once, the mixture can separate, or curdle. The recipe will tell you just what to do.

Mixing in egg whites

1 To mix beaten egg whites into a cake mixture, use a metal spoon. Move it carefully through the mixture, making the shape of a number 8.

2 Mix as gently as you can, to keep the mixture light. Stop as soon as the egg white is mixed in.

Removing cake pans

To remove a cake from a springform cake pan, put the pan over a full food can. Press the sides of the pan down, then, slide the cake off the base onto a plate.

To remove a cake from an ordinary pan, take a plate that's larger than the cake. Hold it over the pan. Turn the pan and plate upside down together. Shake the pan, then remove it.

Stenciling patterns

1 Find a lacy doiley that's a little bigger than your cake. Or, make your own stencil by cutting shapes from a piece of paper that's bigger than your cake.

2 Put the stencil on the top of the cake. Stick a few toothpicks through the holes in the stencil, to keep it in place.

3 Sift some powdered sugar over the stencil and the cake, until it makes a thin, white layer. Then, remove the toothpicks and, very carefully, lift off the stencil.

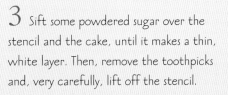

Chocolate muffins

Ingredients:

1 cup + 2 tablespoons semisweet, milk
or white chocolate chips (you could
use allergy-free chocolate)

2½ cups self-rising flour

1½ teaspoons of baking powder

¼ cup unsweetened cocoa powder

½ cup sugar

½ cup vegetable oil

1 cup milk or soy milk

1 large egg

1 teaspoon of vanilla extract

You will also need a 12-cup
muffin pan and 12 baking cups

Makes 12 muffins

Muffins are one of the easiest types of cake to make. All you have to do is mix the liquid ingredients into the dry ingredients, then bake the batter. The main recipe here uses chocolate batter and chocolate chips, but there are instructions for other flavors too.

1 Preheat the oven to 400°F. Put a baking cup in each cup of the muffin pan.

2 Sift the flour, baking powder and cocoa into a large bowl. Add the sugar and chocolate chips. Stir everything together.

3 Measure the oil and milk in a measuring cup. Break the egg into a cup and beat it with a fork. Put it in the measuring cup, along with the vanilla.

4 Pour the milk mixture into the bowl. Mix everything together quickly with a fork. Stop when there are no pockets of flour left.

5 Divide the batter between the baking cups and put the pan in the oven. Bake for 20 minutes, or until the muffins are raised and firm.

6 Leave the muffins in the pan for 10 minutes. Put them on a wire rack to cool.

Chocolate & orange muffins

Extra ingredient: 1 orange. Grate the zest from the orange on the small holes of a grater. Squeeze the juice from the orange. Follow steps 1-2, adding the zest in step 2. In step 3, when you measure out the milk, put back 2 tablespoons of it and add 2 tablespoons of the orange juice instead. Then, follow steps 4-6.

Lemon & white chocolate muffins

Replace the cocoa powder with 1 lemon and ¼ cup extra self-rising flour. Use white chocolate chips. First, grate the zest from the lemon on the small holes of a grater. Cut the lemon in half. Squeeze the juice from one half. Follow step 1. In step 2, leave out the cocoa and add the extra flour and the zest. In step 3, when you measure out the milk, put back 2 tablespoons of it and add 2 tablespoons of lemon juice instead. Follow steps 4-6.

Vanilla & fruit muffins

Replace the cocoa powder and chocolate with ¼ cup extra self-rising flour, ¼ cup extra sugar and 1½ cups fresh or frozen blueberries or raspberries.

Follow step 1. At step 2, leave out the cocoa and add the extra flour, sugar and berries. Follow steps 3-6. If you use frozen berries, there's no need to defrost them.

173

Apple spice cake

Ingredients:

2 medium-sized sweet apples

½ cup + 1 tablespoon of vegetable oil

¾ cup sugar

3 large eggs

¾ cup raisins or golden raisins

¾ cup whole-wheat flour

¾ cup self-rising flour

1½ teaspoons of baking powder

1½ teaspoons of baking soda

1½ teaspoons of ground cinnamon

1 teaspoon of ground ginger

For the topping:

2 tablespoons of raw sugar

½ teaspoon of ground cinnamon

You will also need a 7 x 11 inch
rectangular cake pan

Makes 1 cake

This moist cake is full of raisins, spices and soft apple pieces, and has a crunchy cinnamon sugar topping.

You can adapt this recipe to make carrot cake too — just follow the instructions at the bottom of the page opposite.

1 Heat the oven to 350°F. Line the pan with parchment paper (see page 161).

2 Cut each apple in half. Put the halves flat side down and cut them in half again. Then, cut out the cores (see page 11).

3 Throw the cores away. You don't need to peel the apple quarters. Just cut them into bite-sized chunks.

4 Put the oil and sugar in a large bowl and beat them for a minute with a wooden spoon.

5 Crack one egg into a cup and beat it with a fork. Add it to the oil and sugar mixture and beat it in well. Do the same with the second egg, then the third egg.

6 Put the chopped apple and raisins in the bowl and stir to mix them in well.

7 Sift both types of flour, the baking powder, baking soda, cinnamon and ginger over the mixture. If there are any pieces of bran left in the sieve, pour them in too.

8 Gently fold everything together with a metal spoon, moving it in the shape of a number 8. Scrape the mixture into the pan and smooth the top.

9 To make the topping, mix together the raw sugar and cinnamon. Sprinkle it over the cake. Bake the cake for 45 minutes until raised and firm. Leave in the pan for 10 minutes to cool.

10 Hold the pan upside down over a wire rack. The cake should pop out. Peel off the parchment. When the cake is cool, turn it right-side up and cut it into squares.

Carrot cake

Replace the apples and raisins with 2 medium carrots and ⅔ cup walnut or pecan pieces (optional).

Follow step 1. Grate the carrots on the large holes of a grater. Follow steps 4-5. At step 6, add the carrot and walnuts or pecans instead of the apple and raisins. Then follow steps 7-10. Contains optional nuts.

Sponge cake

Ingredients:

For the cakes:

1½ sticks (¾ cup) softened butter

1 cup sugar

4 large eggs

1 cup + 2 tablespoons self-rising flour

For filling two large cakes:

1½ cups heavy or whipping cream (optional)

4 tablespoons of jam or lemon curd

You will also need:

two 8 inch round, shallow cake pans (to make one big cake) or one 12-cup muffin pan and 12 baking cups (for 12 cupcakes)

Makes 1 sandwich cake or 12 cupcakes

Quick sponge cake

Replace the butter with 1½ sticks (¾ cup) soft margarine or dairy-free spread.

Follow step 1. Sift the flour into a large bowl. Add the margarine or spread and the sugar. Break the eggs into a cup, then add them too. Beat with a wooden spoon until the mixture is smooth. Then, follow steps 5-11.

The main recipe here is for a traditional, light sponge cake, made with butter. You can use this recipe to make a large sandwich cake or a batch of cupcakes. But if you'd like to try a quicker version, using margarine or dairy-free spread instead of butter, follow the instructions below, on the left.

1 Preheat the oven to 350°F. Line the pans with parchment paper (see page 161) or put the baking cups in the muffin pan.

2 Put the butter and sugar in a large bowl and mix them together. Beat them with a spoon very quickly until you have a smooth mixture.

3 Break one egg into a cup and beat it with a fork. Add it to the large bowl and beat the mixture to mix it in well. Do the same with the other eggs, beating well each time.

Move the spoon in the shape of a number 8.

4 Sift the flour into the bowl. Mix the flour into the egg mixture very gently, using a metal spoon.

5 Divide the mixture between the cake pans or the baking cups. Smooth the top of the mixture with the back of the spoon.

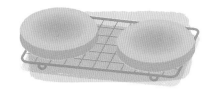

6 Put the cakes in the oven. Bake cupcakes for 15 minutes, or big cakes for 20. Test them, to see if they are cooked.

7 When the cakes are cooked, leave them in their pans for 5 minutes. Then, remove them from their pans and put them on a wire rack to cool.

8 If you're filling a big cake, pour the cream into a big bowl. Whisk it quickly until it becomes very thick and stays in a floppy point when you lift the whisk.

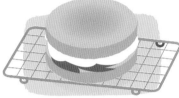

11 You could sift a little powdered sugar over the top of your cakes. Or, cover them with icing (see page 164).

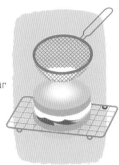

9 Put a big cake with the flat side up. Spread the jam or curd over it, then spread the cream on top.

10 Put the other cake on top, flat side down. Press the cakes together gently.

You could stencil a powdered sugar pattern on your cake (page 171). If so, put the top layer flat side up.

Lemon drizzle cake

Ingredients:

3 lemons

1½ sticks (¾ cup) softened butter, margarine or dairy-free spread)

¾ cup superfine (baker's) sugar

3 large eggs

1½ teaspoons of gluten-free baking powder

1¼ cups + 2 tablespoons fine cornmeal

3½ tablespoons of granulated sugar

You will also need an 8 inch round springform cake pan

Makes one cake

This tangy cake is drizzled with lemon syrup to make it moist and sticky. The recipe contains cornmeal which gives the cake a nice, crumbly texture.

You can also adapt this recipe to make a chocolate cake and cover it in chocolate frosting — just follow the instructions on the opposite page. Both cakes are wheat- and gluten-free, and you can make them dairy-free, too.

1 Preheat the oven to 375°F. Line the pan with parchment paper (see page 161).

Try not to grate any of the white pith.

2 Grate the zest from the lemons, using the fine holes on a grater. Put the zest in a large bowl.

3 Cut the lemons in half and squeeze out all the juice. Put the juice in a measuring cup.

4 Put the butter or spread and the superfine sugar in the bowl with the zest. Stir them together, then beat quickly until the mixture is pale and fluffy.

5 Break an egg into a small bowl and beat it with a fork. Add it to the large bowl and mix it in well. Do the same with the other eggs, too. Beat the mixture well each time.

Stir with the metal spoon, making the shape of a number 8.

6 Put the baking powder and cornmeal in the bowl. Add 1½ tablespoons of the lemon juice. Mix all the ingredients together gently with a metal spoon.

7 Scrape the mixture into the pan and level the top with the back of the spoon. Bake for 40 minutes.

8 While the cake is cooking, put the granulated sugar in the measuring cup with the rest of the lemon juice. It will make a grainy syrup.

9 Take the cake out of the oven. If it looks firm and brown, it is cooked. If not, put it back in for another 5 minutes.

10 Stir the sugar mixture, then pour it over the hot cake. Leave the cake in the pan to cool. When it's cold, take it out of the pan (see page 171).

This cake is drizzled with syrup, so it has a crunchy, sugary topping.

Chocolate cake

Replace the lemons and granulated sugar with 6 tablespoons unsweetened cocoa powder and 1 teaspoon of vanilla extract. Follow steps 1, 4 and 5. In step 6, use just 1 cup + 2 tablespoons of cornmeal, leave out the lemon juice and add the vanilla and 1 tablespoon of water. Follow steps 7-9. Leave the cake to cool, then remove the pan.

Chocolate frosting

You will need ⅔ cup + 2 tablespoons semisweet chocolate chips (or dairy-free chocolate chips), ¾ stick (6 tablespoons) butter or margarine (or dairy-free spread) and ¾ cup powdered sugar. Put the chocolate chips in a heatproof bowl with the butter or spread. Follow steps 2 and 4 on page 162 to melt the mixture. Sift the powdered sugar into the bowl and stir to mix it in. When the cake is cool, spread on the frosting.

Raspberry cupcakes

Ingredients:

For the cake:

2 large eggs

¼ cup + 2 tablespoons superfine (baker's) sugar

1 cup almond meal (ground almonds)

½ teaspoon of baking powder (you could use a gluten-free type)

For the topping:

1 cup powdered sugar

1½ cups fresh raspberries

You will also need a 12-hole muffin pan and 8 baking cups

Makes 8 cupcakes

These light, moist cupcakes are made from whisked egg whites and almond meal (ground almonds), topped with raspberry icing and fresh raspberries. There's also an orange-flavored version. These cakes are gluten-free but contain nuts.

1 Preheat the oven to 325°F. Put a baking cup in each cup of the muffin pan.

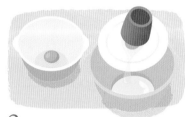

2 Separate the eggs (see page 57), so all the whites are in one bowl and all the yolks are in another.

3 Put the sugar in the bowl with the egg yolks. Use a fork to stir the sugar into the yolks until it is all mixed in.

4 Beat the egg whites very quickly with a whisk, until they become very thick and foamy. Lift up the whisk. If the foam stays in a point, you have whisked it enough.

5 Scrape the egg whites into the bowl with the egg yolk mixture. Mix them in very gently with a metal spoon, stirring it in the shape of a number 8.

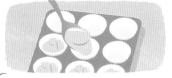

6 Add the almond meal and baking powder and stir them in gently, still using the metal spoon. Divide the mixture between the baking cups.

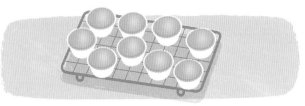

7 Put the pan in the oven and bake for 20-25 minutes, until the cupcakes are raised and golden brown. Take them out of the oven. Leave for 10 minutes, then move them to a wire rack to cool completely.

8 To make the topping, put the powdered sugar in a strainer over a bowl. Shake the strainer so the sugar falls through. Squash any lumps through with the back of a spoon.

9 Put 4 raspberries in the strainer. Squash them with the back of a spoon, so the juice goes through into the bowl and the seeds stay in the strainer. Scrape off any juice clinging to the back of the strainer and put that in the bowl too.

10 Put a teaspoon of warm water in the bowl. Mix everything together to make a smooth paste. You may need to add a little more warm water. If so, add it half a teaspoon at a time and mix it in well before adding any more.

11 Use a small spoon to spread some icing on top of each cupcake. Then, arrange the remaining raspberries on top of the icing.

Orange cupcakes

Replace the raspberries with 2 oranges. Follow steps 1-8. Cut one orange in half. Squeeze the juice from one half. Mix 1½ tablespoons of the juice with the powdered sugar. Spread the icing on the cakes. Cut the remaining orange and a half into pieces (see page 11). Pat the pieces dry with paper towel, then put them on the cupcakes.

What should I eat?

Cooking for yourself using fresh food is much better for you than take-out, or prepackaged meals, and junk food such as hamburgers, fries and sweets. But it's also helpful to know a little about the different types of food there are. These pages will give you some basic information and some tips about cooking for people who can't eat certain things, too.

I can't eat that!

Some people can't eat certain foods because they are allergic to them, or for religious or other reasons. Foods people may need to avoid include dairy products, eggs, nuts, wheat and other grains that contain a substance called gluten, and some types of meat and seafood.

This book is arranged to help. Many recipes have tips for ways to substitute or leave out some ingredients. You'll find these in the introductions or ingredients lists, or in boxes next to the recipes. There's also an allergy index. There you'll find a list of recipes that contain nuts. You'll also find lists of recipes with wheat- and gluten-free options, dairy-free options and egg-free options.

Check your ingredients

If you're cooking for someone with allergies, check the labels of any ingredients such as bouillon cubes, margarine, bottled sauces, baking powder, vinegar, cocoa, chocolate and so on, in case they contain something the allergy sufferer can't eat.

Some ingredients make good allergy-free substitutes. You can use wheat- and gluten-free 'tamari' soy sauce instead of ordinary soy sauce. You can also buy gluten-free and dairy-free bouillon cubes and baking powder. Some dairy-free spreads are fine for cooking, but it's best to avoid low-fat types.

Food types

Different types of food contain different nutrients, which do different jobs in your body. You need to eat a variety of types of food to make sure you are getting a good range of nutrients. This is known as a balanced diet. To help people plan a balanced diet, nutritionists divide food into the 5 groups shown below. You should eat most from groups 1 and 2 and least from group 5. You can see this in the pie chart on the right.

1 Bread, potatoes, rice, pasta & cereals

These foods contain lots of carbohydrates, which give you energy. There are two types of carbohydrates: starchy and sugary. Starchy ones are better for you than sugary ones. Bread, pasta, potatoes, rice and cereals contain starchy carbohydrates that keep you going. Try to include one portion of starchy food with every meal you eat.

2 Fruits & vegetables

Fruits and vegetables contain lots of vitamins and minerals that can help you to fight germs, grow and use the energy you get from food. They also contain fiber, which is vital for keeping food moving through your body and preventing diseases. Eat at least five portions of fruits and vegetables a day. Canned or frozen fruits and vegetables, dried fruits and natural fruit juice count, as well as fresh fruits and vegetables.

3 Meat, fish, eggs, nuts, beans & lentils

Eat two or three portions of these a day. They provide protein, which helps you to grow and allows your body to repair itself.

4 Milk, cheese & yogurt

These foods contain calcium, a mineral that makes your bones and teeth strong – especially important when you're young and growing. Eat two or three portions a day.

5 Foods containing fat &/or sugar

These include cakes, carbonated drinks, ice cream, chips, French fries, cookies, pastries, candies and chocolates. Don't eat too many of these. Your body needs a certain amount of fat to keep you warm and protect the organs inside you, but too much fat can be dangerous. And if you eat too much sugar it can cause health problems, too.

INDEX

For allergy information, see the
Allergy Index on pages 189-190.

If you see (v) after a page number it
means the recipe is vegetarian;
(v options) means you'll find
vegetarian options on those pages.

ALLERGY INDEX

Here you'll find lists of recipes that are dairy-free, egg-free or wheat- and gluten-free, or include allergy-free options. There's also a list of recipes that contain nuts, or things nut-allergy sufferers might not be able to eat — but check these recipes, as nuts are usually optional.

RECIPES CONTAINING NUTS

RECIPES WITH DAIRY-FREE OPTIONS

Edited by Jane Chisholm   Art Director: Mary Cartwright   Digital imaging: Nick Wakeford
Additional design: Anna Gould
Nutritional advice: Alison McLaughlin, MSc, RPHNutr
Every effort has been made to trace the copyright holders of material in this book. If any rights have been omitted, the publishers offer to rectify this in any subsequent editions following notification.